PRUDENCE

CHOOSE CONFIDENTLY, LIVE BOLDLY

FR. GREGORY PINE, O.P.

Our Sunday Visitor
Huntington, Indiana

Nihil Obstat
Msgr. Michael Heintz, Ph.D.
Censor Librorum

Imprimatur
✠ Kevin C. Rhoades
Bishop of Fort Wayne-South Bend
November 8, 2021

The *Nihil Obstat* and *Imprimatur* are official declarations that a book is free from doctrinal or moral error. It is not implied that those who have granted the *Nihil Obstat* and *Imprimatur* agree with the contents, opinions, or statements expressed.

Except where noted, the Scripture citations used in this work are taken from the *Revised Standard Version of the Bible — Second Catholic Edition* (Ignatius Edition), copyright © 1965, 1966, 2006 National Council of the Churches of Christ in the United States of America. Used by permission. All rights reserved.

Every reasonable effort has been made to determine copyright holders of excerpted materials and to secure permissions as needed. If any copyrighted materials have been inadvertently used in this work without proper credit being given in one form or another, please notify Our Sunday Visitor in writing so that future printings of this work may be corrected accordingly.

Our Sunday Visitor Publishing Division
Our Sunday Visitor, Inc.
200 Noll Plaza
Huntington, IN 46750
1-800-348-2440

ISBN: 978-1-68192-732-9 (Inventory No. T2603)
1. RELIGION—CHRISTIAN LIVING—CALLING & VOCATION.
2. RELIGION—CHRISTIAN LIVING—PERSONAL GROWTH.
3. RELIGION—CHRISTIANITY—CATHOLIC.

eISBN: 978-1-68192-733-6
LCCN: 2021953270

Cover and interior design: Lindsey Riesen
Cover art: Shutterstock

PRINTED IN THE UNITED STATES OF AMERICA

Contents

1

Am I Happy?

W ould you describe yourself as perfectly happy? Perhaps you'd say you are somewhat happy or happy enough, but not especially so. We often get the general impression that lasting happiness is far-off, practically impossible, not to be hoped for in this life. And, when someone does describe himself as happy, we suspect him of being naive, like a Midwesterner just arrived in the big city; or unmotivated, like a high school dropout without the least bit of ambition.

When we are made to confront our own unhappiness, it can be distressing, especially when contrasted with the good life proposed in the Gospel. Time and again, we hear it preached: The Lord promises surpassing happiness to those who come after him. "I came that they may have life, and have it abundantly" (Jn 10:10). And yet, very few people seem to enjoy this abundant life. Made suspicious by this apparent contradiction, many of us set aside the work of truly being *happy*, and instead content ourselves with simply being *busy*.

I think here of my first few years of religious formation. I joined the Dominican Province of Saint Joseph in the Eastern United States. After novitiate and profession of simple vows, we do our philosophical and theological formation in Washington, D.C., at the Dominican House of Studies. Though my time at the House was very good and formative, I found myself thinking of happiness as something that came only with solemn vows or ordination or first assignment. I could hope for happiness, but only at a later date. This thought informed my approach to life generally and studies especially.

In my province, it's possible for a friar to shave a year or two off his initial studies, depending on what he did previously and how much work he's willing to shoulder. When I got wind of this, I studied some things on my own, tried to arrange courses efficiently, and generally busied my thoughts with working quickly toward completing my degrees. I thought often and anxiously of expediting the process. And, I'm embarrassed to say, I adopted this mindset without much reflection at all.

At one point though, I was trying to figure out some scheduling problem, and I solicited the advice of another friar. Instead of encouraging me in my pursuit, he called into question my whole project. "Why do you want to rush through?" he asked. Confounded by his challenge, I stumbled in search of an answer: "So I can move on to the next thing and be of service to the people of God," I ventured. Without hesitation, he rejoined, "What about this thing? Isn't this meaningful? Isn't this of great service to the people of God?"

Yikes. Such sense. I was shaken by the incisiveness of his rebuke. I suppose I had just never thought about it in those terms. I was so used to thinking about happiness as deferred satisfaction that I had neglected to think about the purpose and import of what happens *now*. I had failed to engage with the question of happiness as a present reality and, in the process, had just gotten really busy.

I do not think that my experience is an isolated one. Instead of seeking to be truly happy and arranging our lives accordingly, many of us have chosen to be busy. It's become the default response in any conversation: "How are you?" "Busy!" "So busy!" "Crazy busy!" But, upon hearing this response for the umpteenth time in a day, the question that naturally arises is "Why?"

There are, indeed, some legitimately and inescapably busy people in the world; but there are also quite a few of us who just choose to be so, who fill our lives with activity of whatever sort. Kids play multiple sports a season, only to prove mediocre at all of them. Young professionals work long hours, amassing vacation time they'll never use. Older folks find they are incapable of leisurely retirement and slowly accumulate diversions until their days are, once again, full.

Why is this the case? There are any number of reasons for why we overcommit. It could be that we want to be the person who does *all the things* (whether we are being magnanimous or proud). It might be that we're very competent and figure someone else won't do the job as well (whether we are being high-handed or sacrificial). Whatever the reason we give though, the source of our frenzied activity probably runs deeper. Many of us, I suspect, take on so much because we feel like we need to in order to justify our existence. Here we are, feeling a bit unfulfilled and lost. We had hoped that life would amount to more, but it hasn't. With this recognition comes a sadness. It's not so much depression as a kind of existential ache:

It's 10:45 a.m., and I've already had my second thought of lunch. Am I hungry or just anxious?

I'm driving to work, and my phone inexplicably conks out; I can't make calls, and I can't listen to podcasts. Am I bored or just sad?

My friend cancels our evening plans, and I immediately seize the opportunity to catch up on house cleaning, chat with my brother, and watch a show. Am I efficient or just terrified of being alone?

In these moments, how often am I content to wait, to think, and to register the experience? How often do I simply refuse to do so? With the wordless intuition that my life might be a bit light on meaning, I find it far easier to engage in feverish activity rather than to sound the depths of my solitude. So I come to fill my days with busyness because I am afraid. By fragmenting my life — parceling it out among myriad tasks — I barely keep at bay the creeping suspicion that maybe none of this matters.

Real Life Is Elsewhere

All of this running around distracts us from the truth of our lives. Alternately perturbed and paralyzed by our inability to do anything significant, we give up on being real protagonists in the drama of our existence. Instead, we become mere observers. This, at first, seems counterintuitive. You'd think that all our activity would have us feeling more engaged and more empowered. Instead, the opposite proves to be true. We often end up feeling trapped by overcommitment and prevented from taking on more meaningful tasks.

True enough, I finished all my work for the week, but it took most of Sunday afternoon and evening, and I haven't picked up a good novel in three months.

Yes, I was happy to help with organizing the parish festival all weekend, but I didn't carve out any prayer time for three days, and I just feel tired and sad.

Sure, I'm almost done fundraising for my mission trip, but I didn't visit my grandmother in the hospital again this week, and I've been putting her off now for a while.

Rather than really taking hold of our life, it feels like things just sort of happen to us. We get swept along by other people, caught up by their stronger wills and whims. We can't say no, and so we say yes, but under duress and with the secret hope that whatever it is gets canceled.

Looking out over this landscape, we may be tempted to believe that "real life is elsewhere." Whatever this is before me, this is not real life. It is arbitrary. It is accident. My genuine self and my genuine experience lie somewhere on the other side of the present moment. These things here are to be gotten over, to be gotten under, to be gotten around. If I end up learning something, it will be in spite of them, not from them. The devil may be in the details, but God surely isn't.

To make matters worse, this attitude of escape is often paired with a kind of magical thinking about the future. "Sure, things may be rather bleak now, but in days to come it will look different." "Once I graduate, then I can kick the drinking habit." "Once I secure a promotion, then I can get myself on better financial footing." "Once I hit thirty, then my spiritual life will take off." "Once I get married, then I'll be happy."

Think about how this dynamic might play out in the life of an ambitious high school student. At the beginning of her freshman year, she has all kinds of activities to choose from. She may feel motivated to contribute or determined to build her resume; maybe she just feels pressured by friends. Regardless of the reasons, she signs up for sports, orchestra, student government, quiz bowl, French club, and youth group. She takes on practically everything she can shoulder. Freshman year doesn't prove too taxing, but shortly thereafter, her responsibilities begin to overwhelm her. She tells herself that she'll simply see it through so that she can get into a good college with a good scholarship, and *then* she'll pare down to what she truly loves. She stays the course through graduation and breathes a sigh of relief. Time to really live life, right? But what about the reputation she's established for herself? What about the conditions of her scholarship? What about graduate school admission? When the university activity fair rolls around, she finds herself going in for all the same things as before. It's as if she can't help herself. She's become the type that can't not overcommit. True happiness will have to wait. For the present, she'll just have to be busy.

And so, many people find themselves adrift: strangely discontented with the present, groundlessly hopeful for the future, entirely unclear as to how to get from here to there, and all jumbled up by a flurry of activity. At a certain point though, the habit becomes untenable. Though I may have learned to content myself with a life that is dispersed and disintegrated, thoughts of something more continue to crop up. This is not the "abundant life" promised by the Lord. In fact, this isn't anything like what I imagined. What is to be done?

> In the end, real life is not elsewhere. It is *here* and *now*, and its true meaning needs to be first discovered and then pursued.

Rather than look abroad for some self-help scheme to make sense of life, Catholic tradition instructs us instead to return to the very things from which we have been averting our gaze. In the end, real life is not elsewhere. It is *here* and *now*, and its true meaning needs to be first discovered and then pursued. It's not just the externals that need adjusting (weight loss, job security, state in life). Nor is it the cast of characters that needs replacing (housemates, work supervisor, on-again-off-again boyfriend). Those changes mean little without an interior transformation. Ultimately, I'm the one who has to change my approach toward the meaningful things that fill my life, and I won't be happy until I do.

The Search for Meaning

In the last century, a man named Viktor Frankl recognized the importance of acknowledging and embracing the meaning of life. Frankl was a Jewish doctor trained in neurology and psychiatry, just beginning his career in the 1930s. When war broke out, he had the opportunity to flee to America, but he decided to stay in Vienna with his family. By the end of the war, his father, mother, brother, and wife had all been killed either in Jewish ghettos or concentration camps. Frankl, too, was sent to a concentration camp — to Auschwitz — but he somehow made it out alive.

While imprisoned there, he became interested in the question of who survived and how. He was surprised to discover that the physically robust prisoners didn't always last long, but the scrawny ones sometimes hung on with great tenacity. In the end, what he found was that those who had something to live for fared best, and those who didn't fared worst.

Frankl came to believe that a meaningful pursuit was absolutely essential. Whatever the hope one cherished, whether big or small (love for one's children, lingering memories worth preserving, a talent to be used), those who had a purpose were able to fight tooth and nail. As long as a man held that meaning before his mind's eye, he was free to determine his attitude and proceed with resolve. For Frankl, his purpose was tied to the thought of his wife — a fact that he realized one day while walking to his work detail. In his book *Man's Search for Meaning*, he writes, "My mind clung to my wife's image, imagining it with an uncanny acuteness. I heard her answering me, saw her smile, her frank and encouraging look. Real or not, her look was then more luminous than the sun which was beginning to rise."

Inspired by his observations in the camp, Frankl went on to pioneer a psychiatric method called *logotherapy*. In his professional practice, he helped men and women overcome mental illness, especially depression, by aiding them to discover a meaning (*logos*) in life. He describes one particularly beautiful encounter of this sort:

> Once, an elderly general practitioner consulted me because of his severe depression. He could not overcome the loss of his wife who had died two years before and whom he had loved above all else. Now how could I help him? What should I tell him? I refrained from telling him anything, but instead confronted him with a question, 'What would have happened, Doctor, if you had died first, and your wife would have had to survive you?' 'Oh,' he said, 'for her this would have been terrible; how she would have suffered!' Whereupon I

> replied, 'You see, Doctor, such a suffering has been
> spared her, and it is you who have spared her this
> suffering; but now, you have to pay for it by surviv-
> ing and mourning her.' He said no word but shook
> my hand and calmly left the office.

Their simple exchange changed nothing about the brute
facts: The man was still without his wife. And yet, the
conversation broke open a world of meaning. His suffering was not without purpose; it was *for* his wife, and so
he could willingly endure it. Frankl had grasped a keen
insight: The human person is made for meaning, and "He
[who] knows the 'why' for his existence … will be able to
bear almost any 'how.'"

Meaning and Happiness

This brings us back to the question of happiness. What
does it mean to be happy, and what exactly does happiness look like? Psychologists sometimes distinguish
pleasure-happiness (*hedonic happiness*) and meaning-
happiness (*eudaimonic happiness*). The former they associate with the positive emotion of meeting needs and desires: for example, the delight you get from a good meal or
a good workout. The latter they associate with long-term
goals and the embrace of difficulty, like the joy you get
from fasting for a specific intention or serving the home-
less at a soup kitchen.

On the surface, it might seem that a life trained exclusively on pleasure-happiness (without consideration of

meaning-happiness) would help one to avoid the difficult parts of human existence and lead to greater contentment. Psychologists, however, have found that long-lasting pleasure-happiness is inextricably bound up with meaning-happiness. A man who pursues mere pleasure, without taking account of meaning, ends up limiting the scope and enjoyment of his pleasure. As Frankl writes, "It is the very pursuit of happiness [pleasure-happiness] that thwarts happiness [taken together]."

Consider how this plays out in a couple's decision of whether or not to have children. At first glance, it might seem infinitely more pleasant not to have children than to have them. No diapers to change, no discipline to administer, no stomach-churning stress. Sounds wonderful, right? Yes and no. Psychologists have found that a lack of meaningful relationships — especially family relationships — is detrimental to the psychological integrity, emotional balance, and overall fulfillment of the human person. In other words, cutting out the responsibilities of family life means missing out on all its mind- and heart-expanding joy. It means missing out on some of the best parts of life. To be happy, therefore, one must want something more than happiness, from which happiness flows. Ultimately, in order to enjoy true and lasting happiness, one has first to discover the meaning at work in his or her life and then set out deliberately in pursuit.

The Goal of Life
So, what then is life about? To what — to whom — will we

entrust our heart? There are plenty of suitors, but only one worthy spouse. For, as we'll find, a human life is a weighty thing, and some goals simply can't bear the burden of our whole heart's love.

Take, for instance, the pursuit of wealth. We often assign great importance to wealth and put tremendous pressure on ourselves to accumulate it. Status and fulfillment seem to hinge on income. But, as it turns out, there's no "enough" with money. You can always own another horse, another mansion, another football team. But the true goal of life must be perfectly satisfying. What is more, wealth is *for* something else. Money is *for* acquiring material goods, and material goods are *for* providing security, comfort, further opportunity. Both money and material goods are means, while the goal must be a true end. Wealth, then, fails as a candidate.

What about physical beauty, athletic prowess, or perfect health? This, again, is a dead end. While bodily life is part of flourishing as a human, it doesn't tell the whole story — or even the most important part thereof. Think of the fantastic basketball player who repeats platitudes about "teamwork" and "coach's plan" in his post-game interviews and makes dubious decision after dubious decision off the court. Sure, his body is in excellent shape, but hasn't he just proven himself to be another dumb jock? There's something of his humanity that is stunted. Bodily perfection is not what life is about.

Others go in for fame, glory, or honor. Here again, the need for recognition and esteem is powerful motivation.

Whether it's the politico angling for office or the insecure coworker struggling to gain acceptance, humans prefer respect to almost every bodily good. The problem is that fame, glory, and honor are only given on account of something else. You can't be famous merely for being famous, except in very rare cases. Fame, glory, and honor are not the goal in themselves; they merely testify that one is approaching some other goal. So, again, look further.

Even "successfully" discerning your vocation isn't the goal. Some of us think that once we're married or ordained or in vows, then we'll have arrived at the end. Unfortunately, though, this misses the precise point of vocation. Marriage, priesthood, and religious life are but means to the goal, but that goal can be pursued before, during, and after you settle on your state of life. The question remains, then, what is the goal of life?

Infinite Desire

It's clear that each of these different options somehow misses the mark. But is that all there is to be said? Do our lives signify nothing? Are we simply set up for perpetual exasperation? Thankfully, no. We are not just cosmic stuff destined for annihilation, nor are we the products of a manipulative God without thought of our happiness. Rather, we are the creation of a God who cares deeply for us, and we are made to share in his divine life on earth and to abide with him forever in heaven.

In fact, the very dissatisfaction that many of us experience in our various pursuits suggests the existence of something else out there — someone else out there — that is truly and perfectly satisfying. That something — that someone — is, of course, God himself, and we can be confident that we have what we need (or will be given what we need) to be happy in him.

By our very nature, we have the basic resources we need to live our lives well. We have bodies in which to engage the material world. We have passions by which to engage our emotional world. Finally, we have intellects and wills with which to engage the intelligible world. The intellect and the will are what set us apart from the beasts, what most define us as humans. They are the way in which we are most made to the image and likeness of God. They empower us to know reality and its Creator, and to love it (and him). Thus equipped, we step into a world of true and good things among which we have to pick and choose.

There's something peculiar about our picking and choosing, though: Our intellect is never satisfied with just *one* limited, knowable thing, and our will is never satisfied with just *one* limited, lovable thing. Having learned that 3 x 7 = 21, we aren't liable to consider the rest of our times tables unimportant. Having tasted our first chicken sandwich, it's almost certain that we'll return for a second. We are made for *all* of reality, and our hunger and thirst for it are practically infinite.

As a result, we are incurably restless. There is always another chocolate cookie to be devoured or another accolade to be earned. We need constant novelty to take the edge off our continual dissatisfaction. It seems, then, that our infinite desire is something of a curse. After all, isn't it to blame for the perennial temptation to busyness? Yes and no. While our infinite desire may nag us with the feeling of unfulfillment, it doesn't force us to seek lower goods and less meaningful pursuits. It is at the root of *all* our meaningful pursuits — even the highest among them — constantly spurring us on in search of what gives genuine peace and withholding satisfaction until we have found it. Our infinite desire is a blessing. It keeps us from settling for anything less than the full grandeur of our high calling as persons made in the image of God.

The seventeenth century Anglican poet George Herbert captures this sense of restlessness-as-blessing in his poem entitled "The Pulley." He writes,

> When God at first made man,
> Having a glass of blessings standing by,
> 'Let us,' said he, 'pour on him all we can.
> Let the world's riches, which dispersèd lie,
> Contract into a span.'

> So strength first made a way;
> Then beauty flowed, then wisdom, honour,
>   pleasure.
> When almost all was out, God made a stay,
> Perceiving that, alone of all his treasure,
> Rest in the bottom lay.

> 'For if I should,' said he,

'Bestow this jewel also on my creature,
He would adore my gifts instead of me,
And rest in Nature, not the God of Nature;
So both should losers be.

'Yet let him keep the rest,
But keep them with repining restlessness;
Let him be rich and weary, that at least,
If goodness lead him not, yet weariness
May toss him to my breast.'

The point is plain. God withheld rest for our good. Restlessness is his gift. If any random thing or experience could satisfy us, we'd run the risk of ignoring the splendor of what awaits us in heaven. If every fast-food combo meal could make us perfectly content, we'd never make it to the eternal banquet. We would "rest in Nature, not [in] the God of Nature" and miss out on all the loveliness that lies beyond the immediacy of sense pleasure. This is why, as Herbert puts it, God "made a stay" by withholding (or delaying) his gift of abiding peace. God has made us "rich and weary" that we might set out in search of him.

This is the real drama of the human condition: We are wayfarers. We are pilgrims. This world is not our home. Our intellects can always be further illumined, and our wills can always be further strengthened. We can't just put up our feet and declare ourselves happy enough with what we have. This life is not a place of arrival. It is a place of departure. There is nothing here upon which we can hang our whole heart's love. There is only one goal and horizon of ultimate meaning for us: We are made for God and "our hearts are restless until they rest in him."

The Goal Is God

Thankfully, we don't have to figure out the goal. It is revealed to us — in creation, in history, in our very nature. The goal is not even a matter of choice. It's in our very DNA, and we can't escape its call. Josef Pieper writes in *Faith, Hope, Love*:

> In the act of being created we are — without being asked and without even the possibility of being asked — shot toward our destination like an arrow. Therefore, a kind of gravitational impulse governs our desire for happiness. Nor can we have any power over this impulse because we ourselves are it.

To be created in the image of God — open to a sharing in God's life — means that our very identity and self-understanding is bound up with the pursuit of God as our end. We may be fooled into seeking lower things *as if* they were our end, whether wealth, bodily perfection, honor, even vocation; but, when taken on their own terms and not directed to God, these lower goals are but impoverished versions of the divine fullness. We are made for God, whether we recognize it or not. No amount of busyness can blot out the claim this vocation has on each and every human person.

Even if paralyzed by indecision or immersed in a sea of activity, the human heart longs for the divine perfection and peace. The point cannot be emphasized enough: God has created us that we might partake of his very inner life. Sometimes when we talk about God, he may sound far-off or abstract. But what lies in store is remarkably present and concrete. His inner life is undivided, whole, perfect, good, infinite, unchanging, eternal, wise, just, and loving — abiding in the communion of Father, Son, and Holy Spirit. God is all of this and more, for he transcends the creaturely limitations according to which we imagine him. And, perhaps most astonishingly, he is for *you*.

God wants you to be happy. He created you for this express purpose. He trains the whole of his attention on securing it.

God wants you to be happy. He created you for this express purpose. He trains the whole of his attention on securing it. He is not looking to trip you up with temptation and trial. He is not waiting at a distance for you to fail. He is working patiently and ceaselessly to draw you to himself who is happiness itself. Your very existence is testimony that God's happiness cannot be contained within the bounds of his divine nature. His happiness brims over and fills creation that it might return to him in praise. In effect, God has a secret too good to keep — the secret of his divine happiness — and he shares that secret in and with you that you might know and love it now and for eternity.

We can be confident that it is possible to seek this happiness always. Everything that we encounter on earth is permitted or willed by God with an eye toward drawing us to him. Present difficulties are not divorced from our happiness, but are mysteriously related to it. As a result, for the present, there is great delight to be enjoyed and great suffering to be embraced. Earth may afford a foretaste of heaven, but it cannot supply lasting happiness. The human heart will only be wholly satisfied when fixed permanently in God.

Life on earth is an exile from the heavenly homeland, and the journey home can be very hard. The difficulty to be endured is not without purpose, though. As Fr. Bede Jarrett writes in *No Abiding City*:

> Pilgrims, travellers, strangers, that is all we be! But we seek a city, whose maker and builder is God — a city that is God Himself. We shall enter within it by His mercy. God Himself shall be our home. Cannot you be grateful for the road though it be rough and uncertain? It does all a road was ever made to do. It takes you home.

Easy, Right?

With the goal established, shouldn't that make life a lot easier and simpler? With God as our end, it seems like the steps to get there should be pretty straightforward: Do the things that God commands or permits or otherwise counsels, and all will be well. You can imagine the zealous convert's initial resolve: When I wake up, I'll choose God! When I go to bed, I'll choose God! Every opportunity in between, I'll choose God! It's that easy, right?

Unfortunately, no. Concrete decisions in real time are more involved than the movements of spontaneous enthusiasm. What about when you get asked on a second date after having only kind of enjoyed the first one? What about when you have to determine whether to take a gap year based on your mother's tenuous employment situation? What about when you fear that your job has you implicated in unethical research? What does it mean to choose God in those situations?

It's true that having God as our goal makes life easier and simpler in a sense, but there are many means to that goal that need to be arranged. Certain things are ruled out (lying, cheating, stealing); certain things are ruled in (sacraments, prayer, penance); and, other things begin to take concrete shape (forgive my father, reconcile with my old roommate, discern my vocation). But a lot of the details still need to be sorted out. So, how does one go about it? That's the point of this book.

If God is the goal, our trajectory toward him needs to shape every dimension of our existence. Life is not about skipping to the back of the book and looking at the answer key. The point is not merely to *end up* well. The point is to *live* well. To that end, we need to be formed for the task at hand. Think of what follows as formation. So, with the path set before us, let's get busy — not "crazy busy," mind you, but busily dedicated to the work of living life well as

God enlightens and emboldens us in our pursuit of him.

Reflect

How do you understand happiness? How does your experience of life to this point compare to that understanding?

What aspects of your daily life would you rather get over, *cooking!* get under, or get around? What obstacles do you experience when seeking to find meaning in difficult moments? How can you address those obstacles?

What do you find most discouraging about being on the way? How can you find encouragement in the midst of your life's pilgrimage? *Kindness, joy of others can never quite get there – always a flaw in reflection I mourn because of my sins.*

2

Am I Able?

E very time we feel inspired to grow in our relationship with God, we find ourselves confronted by various temptations. Some temptations are straightforward
in their logic, attempting simply to distract, disperse, or
delay. Other temptations are more subtle. One is especially deadly. It reasons, "If souls can be made to rely upon
themselves, they will never actually rely upon God." And
so it undermines by apparent encouragement. You might
say to yourself, "I want to become a saint." The temptation
responds, "Just try harder. Make a daily holy hour, go to
daily Mass, pray a daily rosary, find a bunch of tough pen-
ances, read the whole Bible." Or you might decide, "I want
to stop watching pornography." The temptation responds,
"Just try harder. Make up your mind to stop, get an in-

ternet filter, get an accountability partner, downgrade to a dumb phone, begin an exercise routine." Good ideas all, but if undertaken with merely human resources, they are often destined to fail. *Try harder*: a simple appeal with a deadly consequence. For, in the end, trying harder just convinces us more than ever of our own weakness.

The Psalmist sings, "Lead me to the rock that is higher than I" (Ps 61:2). The rock is the goal. The last chapter identified that goal as God but said little about how to reach it. Notice, the rock is "too high for me to reach." If the goal is something out of reach — if simply trying harder will never be enough to reach it — then what's left for us to do? How do we reach a rock too high for us to reach? In the Letter of James we read, "Every good endowment and every perfect gift is from above, coming down from the Father of lights" (1:17). In the quest to reach God, we cannot pull ourselves up by our own bootstraps. We cannot write our own rags-to-riches story and simply include God in the acknowledgments. Reaching God is not a matter of trying harder. Our pursuit of happiness and our growth in holiness is God's work.

In the next chapter and those to follow, we'll take up the question of practical reason (making decisions) and how one goes about becoming a good practical reasoner. If we were to launch immediately into a list of "Ten Tips and Tricks for Better Decision-Making," we would risk thinking of ourselves as self-made men and women; we would risk imagining the virtuous life as a mere matter of self-help. Instead, we will begin where all good Christian thought begins — with God. To grasp the place of prudence in a good and happy life (which is where we're going), we have to see prudence in light of God, creation, redemption, and grace. For, while we may not be able to reach the rock on our own — by God's grace, we can and will.

God's Cosmic Generosity

Think about what your status was before creation. Actually, don't bother, because you can't. Before God created the heavens and the earth (and even the term "before" is clunky, since there was no time) there wasn't even any nothingness to speak of. So, then, this was our status: We weren't even nothing. You can't get poorer than that. By creating us, God looked upon our less-than-nothingness and put something there. He put us there. God looked to his divine abundance, and patterned us on himself, calling us forth from nothing (*ex nihilo*) to be something *unto* him.

How does one account for God's decision to create? There doesn't seem to be sufficient motivation. Before the dawn of time, God enjoyed the perfect fullness of blessed life. He had no need for adoration or assistance. He stood to gain nothing from bond servants or slavish worshipers. There was no human-shaped hole in God's heart. He lacked *nothing*, and no thing could have been added to his all-sufficiency.

Creation, then, is testimony of God's cosmic generosity. By his free choice, God brings a bewildering variety of good things into existence, among which we human beings are numbered. To all things he gives existence. To some things he gives life. To us, he gives even more. Beyond just being and living, we are made for understanding. God gives us (along with the angels) a spiritual nature capable of recognizing his generosity and referring it back to him. We can know and love God. We can behold his handiwork. We can see how he draws us to himself, not from any insecurity on his part, but rather from an infinite goodness. Based on this knowledge, we can have the confidence that God wants us to be happy. There's just no other way to account for his choice. Creation is *for us* who are *for God*, and we make good on God's bestowal of existence, life, and intelligence by acknowledging the gift and responding generously in turn.

Thus, from the outset, we see that God initiates a good work, one in which he is the primary cause — the main protagonist. Creation is not the fruit of created efforts. No amount of trying harder yields a universe. In truth, we receive everything that we are and have from him. If we are to become better thinkers and choosers, it's not by tips or tricks; it is in union with him who thought of us from the beginning and who chose us for himself.

God's Saving Sacrifice

Creation should have been ample testimony of God's love for mankind, and yet our first parents chose against it. Theologians differ when describing why Adam and Eve fell. Some suggest that they turned toward themselves and away from God. Others say that they took exception to receiving their beatitude as a gift. Still others figure that they failed to trust in God's promises. Regardless of which answer best captures the nature of the sin, a common theme emerges — our first parents treated God's original designs as if they were somehow lacking. God poured himself out in creation, providing us with all we needed to flourish, but humanity proved suspicious, weak, and proud.

By original sin, we were despoiled of grace and wounded in our nature. Whereas formerly the intellect was subject to God, the passions subject to the intellect and will, and the body subject to the soul, now a disorderly chaos reigns within. Left to ourselves, we find it only too easy to sin. Sin is simply the choice of something not in accord with our status as sons and daughters of God, something that wounds our relationship with God, self, and others. Saint Augustine defines sin as "any thought, word, or deed contrary to the eternal law." Put in those terms, it sounds pretty unattractive, but in real time, sin is subtle. More often than not, it is a failure to pay attention to or care about something that we ought to. In the moment, we find ourselves preferring a lower good to a higher good and positively excluding the goodness of God's plan.

So that's the situation in which humanity finds itself after the Fall: mistrusting God, living for lower things, floundering in chaos. With God's goodness having been called into question, one might have expected him to scrap his original plans. Why bother with such an ungrateful creature? There seems no point in an endless series of failures. But, rather than push the reset button and wipe out the memory of our betrayal, the God who marvelously created us went on to redeem us in an even more marvelous way.

Some Christian authors describe God's act of creation as a harmonious song. Sin's entry into the world sounds a discordant note that threatens to ruin creation's harmony. Rather than banishing the sinful voice of fallen humanity, however, God re-orchestrates the other parts of creation's song to produce an even richer harmony.

The fact that creation can be marred should not make us think that it is somehow deficient. A lily is beautiful to behold and delightful to smell, but it can easily be destroyed by a lawnmower. Just because a thing can be ruined doesn't mean that it's bad. Crabgrass is a hardy plant, but its resilience doesn't make it better than the lily. The point is that creation's fragility — the fact that mankind could fall from grace and did — provides the space for an even more excellent demonstration of God's power. In the age succeeding the Fall, we see that God can bring good even out of evil.

Again, note the severity of our existential poverty. By sin we offended a God of inestimable dignity, severing our relationship with him and incurring a burdensome debt. We recognize at once the need to make up for that offense, but its weight proves too heavy for us. Left to ourselves, we have only finite resources on which to draw. How then do we atone for our offense, limited as we are by our human nature? No amount of trying will foot the bill.

Much could be said of how God answers this question through salvation history, but nowhere is his response more perfect and clear than in the passion of Our Lord Jesus Christ. At the crux of history, in the fullness of time, God sent his only begotten Son to assume human nature and to suffer, die, and rise from the dead for love of us. Jesus Christ, the God-man, offers to the Father a pleasing sacrifice in human flesh. By virtue of his charity and obedience, he merits for us the reward of eternal life with him. His offering makes up for our fault and repairs the relationship that was ruined by our original parents. In this redemption, Jesus Christ re-creates man and woman in a manner that transcends the limitations imposed by original sin. In creation, God does something good. In redemption, he does something better.

What, precisely, is this something better — this "how much more," to borrow from Saint Paul (cf. Rom 5)? Christ's redemption is not motivated by a naive nostalgia for the days of Eden. It's not a matter of simply reversing the original sin and getting back to where we were. God's plans are wiser than that. He has a richer harmony in mind.

Consider this: In the original dispensation, grace, our created share in God's divine life, would have been communicated with our nature in the ordinary course. When the woman conceived, her child would have enjoyed the life of grace from the first. As God infused the soul of the child, he would have also bestowed his grace and all that comes with it (virtues, gifts of the Holy Spirit, etc.). But, with the loss incurred by original sin, this arrangement ceased, and now each child comes into the world bereft of his original endowment but with a lingering longing for his supernatural destiny. We are born heaven-haunted.

By the Lord's paschal mystery, this way to the life of grace and glory is re-opened, but in a manner that surpasses the original plan. Now, instead of receiving grace as a God-given birthright, each individual Christian is incorporated, one by one, by the Sacrament of Baptism, into the saving sacrifice of Jesus Christ. What originally would have been communicated to the whole of mankind in each and every generation is now communicated singly in the context of an ecclesial and sacramental friendship. And so, instead of returning to Eden, we are ushered into the kingdom of heaven, the very life of Christ.

This turning from sin and turning to God with the infusion of grace at baptism is continually reenacted in the Sacrament of Penance. When we sin, there is a temptation to regret the sin — to wish it undone. We know our sins have wounded our relationship with God, self, and others, and we would like to have them blotted out from memory (and even reality). But the logic of the Sacrament of Penance operates in a different register. In this sacrament, the Christian is not called to cultivate regret, but rather the virtue of penitence. A penitent heart laments and hates sin because it desires a deeper conversion. Penitence inspires the Christian to look back on the past and to acknowledge how Christ is at work even there — permitting sin and incorporating it into a story of yet more perfect love by bringing goodness out of evil. So, too, with the original sin. Humanity's rejection of divine love was tragic, to be sure, but it has served to fasten us all the more to Christ. As the Easter *Exsultet* sings, "O happy fault, which earned so great, so glorious a Redeemer."

"Set me upon the rock too high for me to reach." Our God comes down, in a sense, and does for us what we cannot do for ourselves. "God shows his love for us in that while we were yet sinners Christ died for us" (Rom 5:8). Salvation is not something of our own fashioning nor is it a fruit of our trying harder. Rather, it is an entirely unmerited gift from God, one that he offered once for all, but yet does not tire of extending to us with each passing day.

Incarnation

Our happiness is to be had in God, and if we are to arrive there, it will be by his gracious assistance. What, then, are the concrete means that the Lord gives to conduct us to himself? How does he get us there?

"I am the way, and the truth, and the life" (Jn 14:6). The first means to our salvation is Jesus Christ. God gives us himself. In the Incarnation, the only begotten Son of God takes our human nature to himself, sharing with us in all things but sin. By doing so, he ensures that we can truly meet him — touch him — in every aspect of our human lives. The Lord has a human soul and a human body, a human intellect and a human will, human passions and even human hunger, thirst, and fatigue. He was conceived; he was born; he suffered and died; he was raised and exalted. "For we have not a high priest who is unable to sympathize with our weaknesses, but one who in every respect has been tempted as we are, yet without sinning" (Heb 4:15).

As the one bridge between God and man, Jesus mediates the infinite gap between divinity and humanity, and through his humanity he conducts us into the love of Father, Son, and Holy Spirit. The rock too high for us to reach came down to the ledge where we were standing. There is a yawning chasm of being between God and man; his nature surpasses ours in a manner defying comprehension. In the order of being, we are closer to the nature of a fly than we are to the nature of God. But in the Incarnation, the Lord Jesus emptied himself, drew near to sinful humanity, and brought us up with him into the divine nature. He "set aside" the glory of his divinity to seek and to save the lost, to live among us as one born of woman, to deliver us from destruction and lead us back to God. And, as a result, we believe and hope that we can heal from sin and live with him forever.

When the Scriptures speak of the reason God became man, they speak straightforwardly of our need for deliverance: "For the Son of Man came to seek and to save the lost" (Lk 19:10). But while saving us from sin, the Lord sees fit to bestow on us yet further riches. In his Incarnation, Christ not only reveals his divinity, but he also begins a process whereby he gives us a share in it. It is common in the Christian tradition to speak of the Incarnation as a principle of *deification* or *divinization*, both of which words mean our becoming like God. Saint Peter writes of salvation in just these terms:

> His divine power has granted to us all things that
> pertain to life and godliness, through the knowl-
> edge of him who called us to his own glory and
> excellence, by which he has granted to us his pre-
> cious and very great promises, that through these
> you may escape from the corruption that is in the
> world because of passion, and become partakers
> of the divine nature." (2 Peter 1:3–4)

In short, the goal of human life isn't merely to be kind or
successful or well-regarded. It is to become like God. As
Saint Athanasius writes, "For He was made man that we
might be made God."

The Church and the Sacraments

Jesus Christ is the unique Mediator and perfect means
for bringing mankind to God. There is absolutely nothing lacking to this mediation. That being said, the Lord
himself has chosen to employ further means, other medi-
ations, to perpetuate his presence in time and space well
beyond his earthly life. The Church is one such means
in which we find still further means. God sends his Son,
the Son institutes the Church, in the Church we receive
the sacraments, and from the sacraments we are enriched
with every grace, virtue, and gift of the Holy Spirit. By
grace, virtue, and gifts, we are conformed to the mysteries
of Christ's life given in the sacraments. These mysteries

make us like him and draw us into the communion of the Blessed Trinity. So, if Christ's mediation is sufficient, why the sacraments?

Saint Augustine defines a sacrament as a sacred sign that makes men holy. In each of the seven sacraments, a visible sign is in service of an invisible grace that it communicates for our salvation. By saying that sacraments make men holy, *make* is used here in just about the strongest imaginable sense. The sacraments are not just suggestive symbols. If, for instance, you roll up to a stop sign, the sign doesn't do to your car what it suggests. You could choose to stop or you could roll right through it. Sacraments, by contrast, work in a much stronger sense. A sacrament is like a stop sign that physically stops the believer's car. It actually causes what it signifies. It establishes and strengthens communion with God.

The sacraments accomplish this end in a way that is profoundly *human*. Each human being is made up of body and soul, a profound union of material and immaterial reality. Relying on our five external senses, we start by perceiving sensible things and move to understanding intelligible ones. Smells recall memories. Sights inspire us with wonder. Hearing transmits words and their meanings. In a similar way, the Church's sacraments communicate immaterially what they signify materially. The sacraments use everyday things — water and oil, bread and wine, human speech and touch — and employ them to communicate sublime mysteries. All at once, we are humbled by the ordinary signs and exalted by the extraordinary realities.

The sacraments are also profoundly communal. Parents and godparents bring the child to the baptismal font. Confirmands take the name of a new patron, one of their forebears in the Faith. Holy Communion makes the recipient more powerfully part of the Mystical Body. The evidence is abundant. The sacraments work effectively to solidify the fellowship of the People of God. In every sacrament we receive the gift of God for ourselves, but we are also made more perfectly a member of the Church, partaking more excellently of its communal life and worship.

Here, again, the means are not a matter of trying harder. The Lord saves the Christian through simple signs in the company of believers. The fact of our humility and dependency is communicated in spades. Salvation is not ours to grasp. It is ours to receive — a rock too high for us to reach. It remains for the believer to beg for that gift, and to receive as God sees fit to give it within the life of the Church and her sacraments.

Grace, Virtues, and Gifts

The divine life courses from God through his Christ into the Church and her sacraments. Ultimately, these mysteries are applied in each human heart. Through this great chain of mediation, the tide of divine abundance spills over the bounds of the Godhead and flows over the individual believer, cleansing and illuminating him in his interior life. What is more, this water of divine life permeates the individual believer, getting into all the nooks and crannies of his very existence. This interiorization of the divine abundance is exactly what is meant by grace.

It's impossible to speak of the Christian mysteries without speaking of grace, and so, of course, I've already mentioned it. Time, then, for more clarity. As it's used in everyday speech, *grace* has three basic senses.

1. First, grace refers to one person's positive regard (or love) for another, as when we say that a particular student is in the good graces of her teacher.
2. Second, grace refers to any gift that is freely given. If your work associate goes to Switzerland on a business trip and brings each of the members of your group a bar of delicious chocolate, you might say it was very gracious of him.
3. Third, grace can refer to the thanks rendered for a gift. This actually forms the linguistic connection between grace (*gratia*) and gratitude.

Each of these three senses is at play when we speak about grace in Christian theology. Grace refers to:

1. God's love for the believer, which
2. takes concrete shape in the life of the believer, and
3. moves him or her to render thanks unto God.

In this specifically Christian sense, grace is defined as *the human person's created participation or share in the uncreated life of God*. As a share in the divine life, grace effects the spiritual adoption of the baptized into the household of God, making them truly to be his sons and daughters. By grace, God comes to our souls and takes up a kind of residence, dwelling within them as in a temple, provided we do not commit mortal sin.

Sanctifying grace — a name for grace taken from its enlivening effect in our souls — elevates the whole person by a supernatural habit. Here, we can draw an analogy with health. We say someone is healthy when everything in the bodily organism is as it should be. All the organs — with their inner workings and interrelations — are functioning well. We say someone is sick when this equilibrium has been somehow compromised. Even a small mass or slightly unusual proliferation of cells is enough to render one unhealthy. We wouldn't say, "You know, he's got pancreatic cancer, but otherwise he's healthy as a horse." Health is said of the whole person. Grace is like the health of the spiritual person. By the presence of sanctifying grace in our souls, the supernatural organism — that is, the human person destined for eternal life in heaven with God — is made to function as intended. In every facet of the life of the soul (intellect, will, and passions) grace heals the wounds incurred by sin and grows beyond the limitations of nature.

To this point, I've described grace mostly in terms of *being*. Grace makes us *to be* like God. It makes us *to be* spiritually healthy. But that's not all there is to be said on the matter. Grace also transforms our *doing* by giving rise to virtues. Aristotle defined virtue as a quality of soul that makes one to be good and to act well. A virtue is a habit of the intellect, will, or passions, which empowers us to live in accord with human nature.

In the Christian tradition, we distinguish between *acquired virtues* and *infused virtues*. Acquired virtues are the virtues that we can build up on our own (though without grace we can only do so imperfectly and sometimes not all). These are the "practice makes perfect" habits of ordinary human life. We can acquire the virtue of temperance by refraining time and again from overindulgence, or we can acquire the virtue of fortitude by consistently facing difficulties and fears. By repetition, we acquire a settled disposition of the soul to act for goods that lead to our flourishing.

Beyond acquired virtues, there are also infused virtues, the most notable of which are faith, hope, and charity. Infused virtues are given by God as an interior effect of grace. An infused virtue is not acquired by mere discipline and devotion. Rather, God just pours it (infuses it) into the soul. As with the acquired virtues, the infused virtues make one to be good and to act well, but they do so on a higher plane. Because of their divine origin and higher function, the infused virtues far outstrip the acquired virtues in excellence and efficacy.

The limits of the divine abundance stretch even beyond the virtues. God gives a variety of other interior helps.

The last we will discuss here are the gifts of the Holy Spirit. Like the infused virtues, the gifts of the Holy Spirit — wisdom, knowledge, understanding, counsel, piety, fortitude, and fear of the Lord — are supernatural habits. They inform our intellect, will, and passions, subjecting them to the reign of grace in our lives. The gifts accomplish this work by disposing us to be receptive to God's promptings. You can think about the divine work in terms of a radio transmission. The Holy Spirit is constantly "transmitting" indications of the divine will, but we may not be able to pick them up. We could be on the wrong frequency, or there could be too much interference, or we may not even know how to work the radio. In this image, the gifts of the Holy Spirit are like interior receivers perfectly attuned to the Holy Spirit's transmission. They open to us a world shot through with indications of the divine will.

By the gifts of the Holy Spirit baptized persons become well-disposed to receive and act upon these divine inspirations. It's as if we are carried along by a divine breath or instinct. The gifts allow God to move the baptized person easily and promptly. While the virtues cause us to act in a human mode, the gifts cause us to act in a divine mode. Operating by the virtues is like pulling at a boat's oars and working through the waves of life in a way proper to human ingenuity. Operating by the gifts, however, is like hoisting the sail and being sped along by the divine help. Over the course of a life, the gifts of the Holy Spirit render the believer more and more docile to the divine inspiration and zealous for carrying it out. It is thus

acquired virtue   infused virtue

that we come to the heights of Christian perfection by an ever more mature exercise of the gifts.

Perfection (or, simply, salvation) is just a matter of responding well and generously to God's initiative. Salvation is God's work before it is ever ours. It is wholly beyond our means — a rock too high for us to reach. Though we certainly must exert ourselves in the effort, it's not enough to appeal to our weak and wounded will. If we hope to try harder (or to try at all), it is only by God's grace. Through the abundant testimony of creation and the Incarnation, we know that God is manifestly generous in providing for us. He gives us the Lord's sacred humanity; he gives us the Church; and he gives us the sacraments. He pours grace, virtues, and gifts into our souls, imparting a redeemed and supernaturalized existence. This redeemed way of being human is the proper setting for the choices we seek to make and the prudence we hope to foster. *Our* choice for him stands always under the mercy of *his* choice for us.

Reflect

How do you imagine yourself in relation to God? As his ambassador? As his employee? As his slave? How do the doctrines of creation and redemption challenge that image?

What are some typical ways you think about past sins? With embarrassment? Regret? Self-accusation? What are some ways the Lord is using those sins in your conversion?

How would you define grace in your own words? How often does grace enter into your conscious thoughts about your past, present, and future? What would your life look like if you patterned your day more on the life of grace?

3

Am I Virtuous?

Humans are choosing creatures. We can envision our lives in different ways and choose to live them however seems best. It's a great honor to be creatures that choose, and it's our responsibility to choose well. But that doesn't always make choosing easy. At times, we feel singularly inadequate for the very thing that we are made to do. Choices can be bewildering: You studied graphic design, and here you're being asked about a management situation. Choices can be intimidating: You think you're ready to propose, but can't imagine yourself as a happy husband and father. Choices can be disheartening: You realize a friendship is codependent and destructive, but lack the desire to end it.

Choices are made harder by sin. In addition to depriving us of grace, original sin also wounds our nature.

- First, our intellects are darkened by *igno-rance*. We often aren't fully aware of our reasons for acting, and others' motivations can be yet more opaque.
- Second, our wills are twisted by *malice*. We are consumed with desire for recognition and control and look on others as a threat to our freedom.
- Finally, our emotions are inflamed by *weakness* and *concupiscence*. We find difficult undertakings repulsive and are inclined toward whatever is comfortable and effortless.

With all of this interior tumult, it's no wonder that we experience choice as difficult, a heavy burden to bear. In tough moments, we might be led to wonder: Why couldn't God have made us incapable of failure? Why couldn't he have set it up so that we simply did what we were supposed to do without all of the anguish? Well, God did make creatures like that. Rocks don't choose. Rocks aren't ignorant, malicious, weak, or concupiscent. They're just rocks. The same is true of plants and animals, in their own way. Each fulfills its purpose as a matter of course — whether by gravity, nature, or instinct. Very few people, though, if given the choice between rock or human being, would choose to be a rock. Because, even though we face the prospect of failure in ways that rocks do not, we are far more noble than boulders or pebbles. More ventured, more gained.

Think of St. Teresa of Calcutta. When she left home

to enter religious life, her mother told her to put her hand in the Lord's and to follow him alone; and that's just what she did. When Christ led her to serve the poorest of the poor in a radical way, she was ready. There was no script for what she did, and yet she discovered her "call within a call" and chose it freely. Rocks can't do that. Trees can't do that. Dogs can't do that. Human beings can. Can you?

As we attempt to answer this question, we hold two convictions in mind. First, God has something good in store for us, and he wants us to be happy. Second, he gives us what we need to live up to our calling. Even with these convictions, though, the way forward remains difficult. If we are to consent to and cooperate with his grace, it will mean doing so in a genuinely human way. It will mean choosing well. And, since prudence is the virtue that helps us in a particular way to choose well, consenting to and cooperating with grace will mean growing in prudence.

How then do we work through the difficulty of choice and fashion a coherent life? The traditional Christian response is straightforward: *by growth in virtue.* By growth in virtue one learns to choose well not just once or twice, but consistently and dependably as a matter of character. Virtue makes one *the kind of person who chooses well*, so that choosing well becomes second nature. Virtue frees one to be who he or she is called to be, in accord with God's revelation of himself in Scripture and Tradition.

A Closer Look at Virtue

Saint Augustine defines virtue as "a good quality of mind,

by which a man lives nobly, of which no one can make bad use, which God works in us without us." To say that virtue is a *good quality of mind* is to say that it is a kind of perfection added to, but deeply in concert with, human nature. Just as one can get better at a particular instrument, sport, or profession, so too one can get better at living life in general. Virtue is the type of quality which works this transformation. To say that virtue is the type of quality "by which one lives nobly" and "of which no one can make bad use" fills out the picture. Some qualities have no particular tendency either to good or to evil. If you learn a lot about stocks and bonds, you could use that knowledge to invest ethically or to game the system. If you have a charming personality, you could use that trait to put your friends at ease or to manipulate your acquaintances. But a virtue is directed to good action by its very nature. One cannot be just or courageous or temperate for evil ends. It's absurd. If you were to try to imagine a situation in which one were just in order to steal or seduce, you wouldn't be describing true justice. Saint Augustine's definition concludes by describing its source, "which God works in us without us." This goes back to the discussion of acquired and infused virtues. While some virtues can be acquired over time through repeated action, the greatest of virtues cannot. They are simply infused by God. When a baby girl is baptized, God doesn't take into account what she has done up to that point in her life or whether she is worthy of divine blessing. Instead, God just floods her soul with grace, virtues, and the gifts of the Holy Spirit. They are done in her, without her.

When exercised in daily life, virtue solidifies character. It heals wounded loves and strengthens weak desires so that one can choose the good more freely and enjoy it more fully. As a result, virtue has a humanizing effect. It enables one to become himself in the most genuine sense. In *What Catholics Believe*, philosophers Josef Pieper and Heinz Raskop say this about virtue:

> A good man is more of a man than a bad one, in the sense that he is making more of his humanity. He is in every respect more fit. Thus a man's virtue shows that he is putting his ability into practice; here and now he is making actual what would otherwise remain merely possible within him. This means that he does good — and that he does it not because he has to, but because he wills to. He wants to, and he can.

Virtue fills up and fills out what it means to be a human. It empowers one to be excellently human — to think, to choose, and even to feel well. Ultimately, virtue provides us the tools to live a happy and holy life. A couple of examples will help to illustrate the point.

Temperance is a virtue which heals and elevates the passions of love, desire, pleasure, hatred, aversion, and sorrow. These are simple passions that arise when we encounter something good or evil, causing us either to advance toward the good or withdraw from the evil. Without temperance, we can be easily undone by simple emotional responses. You open a bag of Chex Muddy Buddies and are soon surprised to find there are none left and that you're covered with powdered sugar. The thought of doing something productive is so oppressive that you watch four episodes of a new Netflix series before realizing where the time has gone. When it comes to dealing with sensible things — like food, drink, or sexual intimacy — we need the virtue of temperance to help us cling to our purpose, lest we be swallowed up by lower goods. Temperance puts reason into our passions, so that when looking at a plate of chocolate-chip cookies we can think, "Looks delicious, but I'd prefer not to snack between meals," or "One would be perfect, but I should move on before I have a second," or "Let me pass this around to the guests first." A temperate person has a healthy relationship with sensible goods. He or she is not ruled by them but is able to incorporate them into life in a way that's well-ordered.

Fortitude is a virtue that heals and elevates the passions of hope, despair, fear, daring, and anger. These are more complex passions that arise when we encounter a good that is difficult to attain or an evil that is difficult to overcome. While temperance helped us deal with the plate of cookies right in front of us, fortitude made the cookies possible in the first place when it meant braving a busy supermarket, making the dough without an electric mixer, and timing them perfectly in an erratic oven. Fortitude comes to the rescue in a variety of circumstances. Perhaps all you need to finish off the master's degree is a fifty-page thesis, and you've been stuck at forty pages for the last four months. Fortitude helps you get it across the finish line. Or maybe your boss makes work intolerable with his micro-managerial terrorism, but frankly you're terrified of him and unwilling to confront the situation. Fortitude helps you to speak up. In these circumstances, the good represents the fruit of some struggle, and we are forced to confront our own weakness. To brave these trials, we need the virtue of fortitude so that we're not cowed by fear and turned aside from the goal. Fortitude, like temperance, makes our passions more reasonable so that when God asks for a sacrifice, we can offer it without hesitation; or, when the battle rages on every side, we can stand and fight for love of what is ours. A courageous or brave person has a healthy relationship with difficult goods. He or she is not tossed to and fro but is self-possessed and resolute.

Temperance and fortitude are immediately recognizable to us as good for the human person and as helps in choosing well. How often have you wished you could stop at one cookie or felt unable to tackle a difficult conversation? We know for sure that we can be easily derailed by sense delights or difficulties, and when we are, choosing well becomes infinitely more complicated. With virtues like temperance and fortitude (though we might add justice, humility, chastity, and others), we train ourselves to live more reasonably and so experience less conflict in choice. In so doing, the virtues chart a path to freedom. Virtue makes us persons who choose well and frees us to flourish.

Freedom in Virtue

As we grow in the virtuous life, we become truly free —
free to choose what is good because we love it. St. Thomas
Aquinas, following Aristotle before him, insists that the
point of the moral life goes well beyond restraint or discipline. The virtuous life isn't intended to be a continuous
series of Herculean efforts. Rather, the virtuous life makes
choosing and possessing the good easy, prompt, even joy-
ful. When you see an elite athlete at the top of his game or
a concert musician at the height of her powers, they make
it seem almost effortless. The goal for each of us is to live
our human lives in just this effortless way.

On this point, Aristotle and Saint Thomas highlight
how virtue differs from continence, incontinence, and
vice. Since these are fine shades of moral reality, it's worth
illustrating each state. To that end, take the example of
someone who is deciding whether or not to be honest on
her tax returns. For the virtuous person, it's not even a
question. She reports her earnings accurately and precisely, and she couldn't fathom doing anything else, regardless
of present financial straits. She isn't motivated by fear of
discovery, nor does she think in terms of duty-driven obligation. In fact, she derives a kind of enjoyment from filing.
For the vicious person, again, it's not even a question, but
in the opposite sense. She feels 100 percent entitled to all of
her dollars. If they want to come after her, she'll tell them
the exact same thing. She knows the law and the purpose
of the law; she just doesn't care. She wants the extra cash.

Virtue and vice live at opposite ends of a spectrum. Between them are the two intermediate states of continence and incontinence. Continence is closer to virtue, while incontinence is closer to vice. The continent person experiences conflict or difficulty in her pursuit but eventually succeeds in choosing the higher good. In our example, the woman struggles to balance the ledger, running through different rationalizations why she might report a little less for income or a little more for charitable donations. After some tortured moments, she overcomes the temptation, motivated in part by an ill-defined terror of the IRS, and reports honestly. The incontinent person also experiences conflict or difficulty in her pursuit, but she succumbs to her weakness. That being said, she's not nearly as pleased with her choice as is the vicious person. The choice makes her nervous, and whenever her phone rings, she assumes that she's been found out.

This spectrum of states delineates how human beings can be more or less well-formed in their estimation and pursuit of what is good. The vicious person is malformed. The virtuous person is well-formed. The continent person is on the way and the incontinent person a bit further off. This range of options also helps to clarify the goal of the moral life. Man is made for more than merely following the rules well or performing his duty. He is meant to cultivate a real knack for the good and to incline spontaneously toward it as if by a kind of second nature. By growth in virtue, he develops this facility for living well — for choosing well. To become virtuous is to become a virtuoso at living human life.

Consider a musician. At some point in primary school, whether third or fourth grade, practically half of the class signed up for an instrument rental and music lessons. Our musician was among their number. By the end of the sixth grade, most of her classmates have dropped out, but she persisted. At first it was a bit of a slog, but then she started to get the hang of it. A steady ration of scales, arpeggios, and etudes revealed to her the beauty of the instrument. In time, she advanced from modest pieces to arrangements of increasing technicality. She corrected her initial sloppiness with renewed commitment to posture, technique, and form. Soon, her first tastes of excellence fueled a desire for perfection — for greater artistry and subtlety. Her talent, first encouraged by parental oversight, then grew by its own interior laws. Love of the art inspired her efforts. What began with mastering the rudiments soon had her excelling at and delighting in her craft. The fruit of her discipline was a freedom made visible in both workmanship and flair. She had become a virtuoso — a virtuous — musician.

The example of the musician helps us better to grasp the crucial difference between being continent and being virtuous. A lot of people seem to think that the point of the moral life is continence, as if we were made for a lifetime's toil of scales, arpeggios, and etudes. In fact, the point of the moral life is virtue. We are made for concert performance. We are made to fire on all cylinders and to do so as if effortlessly. Virtue is not a matter of mere moral might; it actually changes us in our inmost being. It makes us *good* and *fit for good deeds.* The virtuous person knows what the good life is and chooses it without hemming or hawing. Virtue empowers us to think, to choose, and to feel well. Virtue frees us for flourishing. This is the vision to hold before your mind's eye as you keep reading. Whether we are focusing on better theory or better practice, it is ultimately to this end. In what remains of the chapter, we will continue advancing toward this goal, homing in on prudence in particular. Before that, though, we'll situate prudence among the different kinds of virtues.

Kinds of Virtues

When listing virtues, the Christian tradition thinks in terms of categories or groups. First, there are the theological virtues: faith, hope, and charity. The theological virtues are called theological because they come from God and go to God. Earlier it was said that some virtues are acquired, while others are infused or received. The theological virtues can in no way be acquired; they can only be infused. Also, when we say that they go to God, this means that they have God as their end — each of these virtues genuinely approaches or arrives at God in some way. Faith adheres to God as First Truth speaking. Hope fastens to God as Final Good promised.

Faith adheres to God as First Truth speaking. Hope fastens to God as Final Good promised. Charity embraces God as First and Best Friend.

Charity embraces God as First and Best Friend. Between their arising from God and returning to God, the theological virtues come to rest in the spiritual powers of the human soul. Faith perfects the intellect, and hope and charity perfect the will. Together, they are considered the greatest of virtues since they come from the highest cause, attain to the highest end, and perfect our highest powers.

Second, there are the moral virtues of justice, fortitude, and temperance. These virtues can be both acquired and infused. There is a lively debate among Catholic theologians on this point, but most hold that the soul can accommodate both acquired and infused versions of these virtues at the same time. So, by acquired temperance, you might concern yourself with dieting for purely natural reasons, whereas by infused temperance you might concern yourself with fasting primarily for the love of God. By contrast to the theological virtues, the moral virtues stay within the limited sphere of human affairs — bringing order to the interior dynamics of sense life and the exterior dynamics of human interaction. Justice perfects the will (rational appetite), and fortitude and temperance perfect the passions (sense appetite). Whereas the theological virtues make one more perfectly like God, the moral virtues make one more perfectly human.

At this stage, you might be remembering grade-school catechism and thinking, "Wait, isn't prudence a moral virtue?" It is and it isn't. Most Catholic theologians teach that moral virtues are found in the appetites, whether in the will or the passions. Prudence is involved with the appetites, but it is really and truly found in the intellect. But because of its close cooperation with the appetites, it plays a double role, bridging the moral virtues and the intellectual virtues. If we are being precise, prudence is an intellectual virtue. There is a way, however, of grouping prudence with the moral virtues. Together, they are called the cardinal virtues. The word *cardinal* is taken from the Latin word for "hinge." Used in this way, it signifies the importance of these four virtues for human flourishing. Together, they are the very "hinges" of the door through which we enter into the fullness of the moral life.

Virtues of the Intellect

That covers theological, moral, and cardinal virtues; only the intellectual virtues remain. Or do they? Often enough, many people are content to leave the intellectual virtues to the side, and some go so far as to caution against them. As Charles Kingsley chides, "Be good, sweet maid, and let who will be clever." But must we choose between intelligence and goodness? The main current of the Christian tradition doesn't think so. In fact, it sees intelligence and goodness as inextricably bound up. The recent popularity of cognitive-behavioral therapy (CBT) has helped raise contemporary cultural awareness to the fact that flourishing is, in part, a product of thinking and knowing well. All virtue bears the mark of reason, and virtue of whatever sort requires a reason that is itself perfected by virtue. Intellectual virtues, especially the virtue of prudence, answer to this need.

The human intellect can be exercised in two different ways. Sometimes we seek to know for knowing's sake. This use is referred to as the *speculative reason*. (Reason just means intellect in this context.) Other times, we seek to know for doing's sake. This use is referred to as the *practical reason*. To be clear, there aren't two reasons, rather there are just two different uses — speculative and practical — of the one reason.

There are three main virtues of the speculative reason: understanding, knowledge, and wisdom. *Understanding* is the habit that discloses the most basic principles of human knowing. Before you even begin to think, you already have an innate capacity for making sense of reality. Understanding is the virtue that registers these fundamental insights — things like, "A whole is greater than any of its parts." *Knowledge* is the fruit of one's judging and reasoning upon reality. It registers necessary conclusions about the world — things like "All men are mortal" and "Whatever is moved is moved by another." *Wisdom* is both the knowledge of the highest things, and the highest mode of knowledge. The wise person has a keen intellectual sense for how all of reality hangs together and is able to know and order all things fittingly.

There are two main virtues of the practical reason: art and prudence. Art is defined as right reason applied to making. Obviously, this covers more than just painting or music. It includes any trade or skill that shapes material reality. Carpenters, athletes, teachers, and poets all qualify. Art, and the artist, is judged good or bad based on whether the thing is well or ill made. The excellence of the artist is not determined by his motive or his sincerity, but by the excellence of his product.

The last virtue standing is the virtue of prudence. You are probably interested in understanding and practicing prudence better; after all, you picked up this book and have read this far. And yet, many people seem to care little for the subject, or at least not enough to read a book about it. Why is that? In part, it's because prudence sounds, to many ears, like a wet blanket. We often think of the prudent person as someone who is shrewd in business dealings. He is a maker of economical arrangements. He is cautious and careful in providing for his own interests. Josef Pieper writes of this modern characterization in *The Four Cardinal Virtues*:

> In colloquial use, prudence always carries the connotation of timorous, small-minded self-preservation, of a rather selfish concern about oneself. A 'prudent' man is thought to be one who avoids the embarrassing situation of having to be brave. The 'prudent' man is the 'clever tactician' who contrives to escape personal commitment. Those who shun danger are wont to account for their attitude by appealing to the necessity for 'prudence.'

Is this all there is to it? Again, the Christian tradition has much more to say on the matter, and limiting prudence to narrow self-interest only obscures its true beauty. The word as it is often used is an impoverished version of the true virtue.

Prudence is right reason applied to doing. It's the habit of intellectual competence or practical wisdom. It's related to what the French call *savoir-faire* or *clairvoyance*. Prudence suggests sagacity or intellectual penetration. It means clear and skillful knowledge of the truth. Importantly for our purposes, prudence plays a decisive role in moral growth. It works to perfect human choice by degrees, helping one to become completely and truly free. Prudence sees to it that our choices are not isolated instances of moral misery, but part of a bigger story of growing in virtue, maturing in freedom, and attaining true happiness.

Prudence sees to it that our choices are not isolated instances of moral misery, but part of a bigger story of growing in virtue, maturing in freedom, and attaining true happiness.

In the virtuous life, the role played by prudence is paramount. Mindful of this, the remaining chapters are devoted to understanding prudence better, so that we can apply ourselves to practicing it better. The hope is that, with a bolstered prudence placed squarely at the center of our moral imagination, we can make strides toward living and choosing well. Because although human life is filled with difficult choices, it is our high calling to see it through. By the grace of God, the prudent person can ascend by choice all the way to genuine happiness. Rocks can't. Trees can't.

Dogs can't. You can.

Reflect

What do you imagine when you think of the life of virtue? Do you feel like you are doomed to a life of boring rule-following or to a white-knuckling climb on the brink of hell-fire? How does this picture of virtue challenge that notion?

Think of someone whom you consider a virtuoso of human life. What marks out his or her life as so wonderful, so admirable? What are some of this person's virtues that you want to incorporate in your own life?

What role does intelligence play in the good life for you? Are you more likely to overthink or to underthink your pursuit of happiness and holiness? How does envisioning the good life in terms of the intellectual virtues help to work through that?

4

Am I Prudent?

The question is all lined up: What is prudence? Specifically, how does it help us to choose well or how does it perfect practical reason? With the goal — happiness — held before our mind's eye, the help of God in ready supply, and the virtuous life to animate our efforts, it's time to start answering the question in earnest. One of the best ways to address this question is by exploring and engaging all of the parts that together make up prudence. By focusing our efforts in this way, we see both how attractive is the life of prudence and how to begin growing in it.

This chapter and the next are a little more philosophical than the last three. If you find the discussion difficult at points, don't be discouraged. Things will make more and more sense as you read on. Think of it as an apprenticeship in prudence as you work your way toward mastery.

Prudence, we have said, is right reason applied to *doing*. It's the habit of acting according to sensible, reasonable standards. It perfects the *practical reason* — the dimension of our reason concerned with knowing for doing's sake. What is more, prudence perfects every imaginable aspect of practical reason. But what are all these different aspects? A good way to proceed is by sketching the different stages or parts of human action and then describing prudence's activity at each stage. Following the clear teaching of St. Thomas Aquinas, we will explore:

- First, the stages of human action, focusing on those stages in which prudence is at work.
- Second, how a prudent act unfolds.
- Third, the different parts of prudence. This section illustrates the different perfections that make up the virtue and gives a detailed picture of how prudence empowers one to know, to choose, and to live well.

Human Action

Typically, when describing a human act, we treat it as a single thing. What did you do? I went grocery shopping. I watched the basketball game. I registered for classes. But each of these acts is made up of a more involved series of smaller steps. Saint Thomas identifies the smaller steps and groups them together in three main stages of human action.

In the first stage of human action, you intend the end. The end is the goal, purpose, or ultimate meaning of the action. For instance, you might choose to diet for any number of reasons — to lose weight, to manage food allergies, to treat anxiety, and so on. Any of these might function as the end of your action. The end is the most important feature of any action, because without it the choice never gets off the ground. Just as there's no sense in preferring vegetables to chocolate-chip cookies without a notion of nutrition, so there's no sense in human action without an end. The end shapes the whole act from start to finish. Though it's the last thing carried out, it's the first thing envisioned. And so, at the outset of any choice, we apprehend (grasp) and intend the end.

In the second stage of human action, you choose the means. Means are just ways of achieving an end. If you intend to diet you have to decide how to go about it. Specifically, what method will you adopt? In certain scenarios, choosing the means will be relatively straightforward. If the diet was suggested to you by a friend who already has a regimen in mind, all that's required is to get on board. If it's up to you to decide, it may be a bit more involved. There are so many different dieting options, and you have to think through, consent to, and ultimately choose the one that is best for you. For instance, there are all kinds of meal options and fitness programs available. Which ones are well-suited to you? Are there certain things you just can't live without? Are there certain workouts that you know you won't or can't do? Are there some challenges you've been hoping for the opportunity to tackle? Are there some life hacks you've just been waiting for the moment to test out? In this process, you gradually home in on a decision, as you advance from what's possible to what's best. At this stage, then, we judge and choose the means of our act.

In the third stage of human action, you use the means. At this point, the choice has been made; it's just a matter of seeing it through. In the first and second stage of action, your choice probably had to mature through thought and conversation. In the third stage of action, it gets fleshed out and translated into bodily movement. No longer are you just intending to diet or choosing a diet, you're really dieting. This doesn't mean that the action's over, though. At this stage, you have to remain engaged — to oversee and direct the choice. It's not as if you have to continually rechoose the means. That's a done deal. But what follows isn't automatic. The choice needs to be continually embodied in practice. With changing circumstances, it can be a real effort to ensure that the act is carried out in the best way. In the case of your diet, perhaps you have some success in your first few weeks, only to plateau for a month. What then? Do you give it up and try something new? Or do you stay the course? Perhaps at this point, you realize that you're beginning to enjoy exercising, which is a promising development. So you add length and intensity to your workouts and don't tinker with anything else. Eventually, the pounds start coming off again. You haven't revised your choice, so much as applied it in new circumstances. At this stage, we execute the action as we command and use the chosen means.

This is the basic template of any human action. At each stage there are paired acts of intellect and will. First, one apprehends (intellect) and intends (will) the end; second, one judges (intellect) and chooses (will) the means; and third, one commands (intellect) and uses (will) the means.

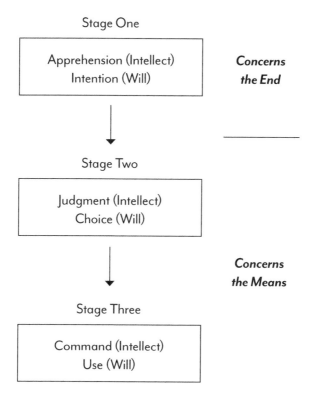

Stage One

Apprehension (Intellect)
Intention (Will)

Concerns the End

Stage Two

Judgment (Intellect)
Choice (Will)

Concerns the Means

Stage Three

Command (Intellect)
Use (Will)

The Three Acts of Prudence

Where does prudence fit in this overview of human action? Prudence isn't directly concerned with the first stage. The ends of human action are supplied by will and passions under the guidance of the moral virtues — how that works will be discussed in the next chapter. Prudence steps in at the second stage, once the end is set. Prudence concerns the choice and use of the means. Once you have apprehended and intended the end of dieting, prudence sees that intention all the way through to weight loss. Prudence is about the means — the "how" of human action.

Saint Thomas identifies three acts of prudence, which he calls counsel, judgment, and command. These three acts map onto the second and third stages of action described above. We have already come across judgment and command. They are the intellectual components of the second and third stages of human action outlined above. But what about counsel, the first act of prudence? Counsel hasn't come up yet explicitly, but it precedes judgment in the second stage of human action. Specifically, it comes to the aid of judgment when there are many means from among which we can choose.

An action may be more or less complicated at the second stage. In a less complicated action, there might be only one means to a particular end. If you want to visit a friend who lives halfway around the world, it may be physically possible to go by foot, bicycle, or train, but the chances that you would actually entertain these options are effectively zero. If you go, you're going to fly. In actions like this, or in the earlier case of dieting when the friend has a regimen in mind, you move right from intention (first stage) to choice (second stage) without an intermediate stage. Many habitual and unimportant choices unfold in this way. You don't agonize about what barber or hair salon to use each time. You just go to the same one. You don't spend much time choosing your route across town. You just follow the GPS.

In a more complicated action though, there might be a few means to a particular end. Say, for instance, you want to travel from Washington, D.C., to New Haven, Connecticut. If you drive, it will take about six hours. You like listening to podcasts and audiobooks, but aren't especially excited to drive alone. If you take the train, it will take about the same amount of time. On the one hand, that would free you up to work en route. On the other, you'd be without a car in New Haven. These two options cost about the same amount and are much more efficient than flying. So what will you do? In choices like this one, and the earlier case of working through the different diet options, you don't move directly from intention to choice. Instead, you pass through an intermediate stage during which you weigh those different options. In the process, certain candidates emerge as more reasonable or more preferable for whatever reason. These options become the fodder for our judgment/choice. This intermediate stage is called counsel (from the vantage of the intellect) or consent (from the vantage of the will). In these more complex human actions, the second stage is composed of two distinct acts — counsel/consent and judgment/choice — which are just the first two acts of prudence. After all that, the third act of prudence is straightforward. It corresponds neatly with the third stage of human action.

Let's trace the workings of prudence through each of its three acts. Counsel is the stage of discovery. It's the point at which we entertain different means, compare them to the end, and size them up against each other. Counsel plays out different possible patterns of cause and effect for the action under consideration to determine which means are most likely to conduct us to the end. So we might ask a variety of questions: Which is easiest? Which is quickest? Which is noblest? Which is most consistent with my character? Which is most likely to make me the man or woman I want to be? There are a variety of helpful ways for thinking through different scenarios. Answering these questions can prove difficult, though, especially if you haven't encountered a similar situation before.

To work toward an excellent choice, certain things have to be in place at the stage of counsel:

- First, the end has to be good. If the end is evil, it's a non-starter. Better to abandon ship than chart a course to destruction.
- Second, the means themselves have to be good. As Saint Paul instructs the Romans, one cannot do evil that good may come (Rom 3:8). A good end doesn't justify evil means.
- Third, counsel has to have a sense of timing. Neither hasty nor halting, counsel aims for

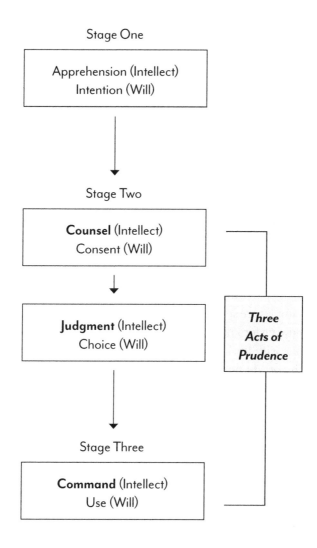

Stage One

Apprehension (Intellect)
Intention (Will)

Stage Two

Counsel (Intellect)
Consent (Will)

Judgment (Intellect)
Choice (Will)

*Three
Acts of
Prudence*

Stage Three

Command (Intellect)
Use (Will)

what is fitting at the proper time.

- Fourth and finally, counsel has to account for the big picture. While a particular means might make sense on its own terms, it must fit in with the whole of one's life. Counsel weighs all of the relevant factors.

From counsel, prudence passes to judgment. In its most basic form, a judgment is just a comparison of two things. That comparison can be expressed in the form of a proposition. For instance, "Penguins exist," or "My brother is not short," or "I shouldn't cheat on this test." In a judgment, one is either composing two things — like penguins and existence — or dividing two things, like my brother and shortness. Judgments, in the broad sense, can be either speculative or practical. The penguin and brother examples are speculative judgments. Both are occasions of knowing for knowing's sake. There's nothing further to be done with the knowledge they supply. Since judgments of this sort do not concern action, they do not engage prudence. Rather, they engage speculative intellectual virtues like knowledge and wisdom.

The cheating example is a practical judgment. In this case, it's an occasion of knowing for doing's sake. There is something further to be done. Here, one doesn't compare a being to its existence or to one of its characteristics. Instead, one compares an abstract principle of human action, like "Evil is to be avoided," with a concrete, particular action under consideration, like "Cheating on this test would be evil." From this comparison, one draws the conclusion, "Cheating on this test is to be avoided" or "I shouldn't cheat on this test." In this example, the judgment moves beyond itself. It is directly ordered to action, and it isn't complete until it shapes and moves the will and passions. Judgments of this sort do engage prudence. They account for prudence's second act.

From judgment, prudence passes to command. Command is the intellectual act at work in the third stage of human action. Command ensures that the chosen means are seen through. It brings our counsel and judgment continually to bear on reality as the action is brought to perfection. It achieves the end of practical reason. Command is the *distinguishing*, *determining*, *culminating*, and *animating* act of prudence.

First, command is the *distinguishing* act of prudence. Whereas counsel and judgment, at times, contribute to the working of other virtues, command is peculiar to prudence. At a certain point, Saint Thomas refers to prudence simply as "the virtue which commands."

Second, command is the *determining* act of prudence. Command is where one's character is brought to bear on reality. On the one hand, command shows the thought that went into a choice and the quality of the person who chose it. On the other hand, it indicates that person's trajectory in life and conducts him or her along that path. Command is the place where one passes from *was* and *is* to *can be* and *will be*.

Third, command is the *culminating* act of prudence.

Command carries with it the power of actual performance of a chosen word or deed. It is immediately concerned with doing since it actually applies the choice. As such, command is able to mobilize the full force of practical reason, that is, knowing for *doing's* sake. We can counsel all kinds of courses of actions and make all kinds of excellent judgments as to how best to realize those plans, but until such time as we actually carry them out, those deliberations and judgments remain incomplete. Command fully applies them to action.

Finally, command is the *animating* act of prudence. In prudent action, we look always to command, to the full embodiment of the action in real time. To aspire to less would be impractical. Counsel is ordered to judgment, and judgment is ordered to command. Command, in turn, draws counsel and judgment to itself, reaching back and shaping all that comes before.

The Eight Integral Parts of Prudence

These three acts — counsel, judgment, and command — sketch a passable likeness of the virtue, but they're really just a scaffolding built around the edifice of prudence itself. What then of the foundation, the walls, the roof, and all that goes into the building? What of the real substance of prudence which makes for the excellent human being, the type we want to be, the sort who would be an irreplaceable colleague, a trustworthy friend, a strong lover of God?

By a closer look at the metaphorical foundation, walls, and roof that together make up prudence, we discover a wealth of subtle perfections, testimony to the divine craftsmanship at work in the life of reason. Saint Thomas calls these perfections the integral parts of prudence. He lists eight of them: memory, docility, understanding, shrewdness, reason, foresight, caution, and circumspection. The common mistake when describing these parts is to think of them as eight moments of prudent action occurring one after another in chronological sequence. This paints an overly neat and potentially misleading picture. Rather than moments, they are perhaps best thought of as bricks in the edifice of prudence. Together, the integral parts work jointly in prudent action to build out the fullness of the virtue.

Saint Thomas divides the eight integral parts into two main groups, based on whether they concern knowing or commanding. The integral parts which concern knowing are memory, understanding, docility, shrewdness, and reasoning. These help with acquiring, retaining, and using knowledge.

The first part of prudence that Saint Thomas treats is **memory**. Memory recalls experiences of the past. In matters of prudence, experience goes a long way. It's for this reason that young people are more likely to lack prudence and old people are more likely to have it. Since prudence concerns practical matters which involve all kinds of particularities and contingencies, it's basically impossible to have a tidy science of decision-making. There's just too much that's up in the air. And so, the prudent person weighs his or her experience of the past and uses that memory to account best for present circumstances. Memory recalls what tends to happen and applies that as best it can.

While it may be helpful for the prudent person to have a vast memory, it's more important that he or she have a profound memory. Some people think that their lives are necessarily enriched by many different experiences, as if you were better for having traveled to Thailand, South Africa, and Norway. But, breadth doesn't always make for depth. When it comes to the memory involved in prudence, it's more important that you experience reality well than that you experience a lot of it. It's a matter of what Josef Pieper refers to as "true-to-being memory." For memory of this sort, it is sufficient that you judge with careful attention, that you seek to retain events and things as they really are.

Saint Thomas gives some advice on how best to cultivate memory of this sort. First, you have to work to retain memory, lest it slip away. This might be by mental association or frequent recalling or journaling. Second, you have to organize your memory. That means finding an orderly place for the things you want to remember, rather than just heaping them up in a pile of random facts. Third, you have to return to it often. If God is teaching through memory, then it merits continual attention. Here, prudence touches prayer. In time with the Lord, there is opportunity to revisit the past, ask for insight, and think through connections, and then anticipate how you might respond again in similar circumstances. This ensures the healthy working of memory.

Take the simple example of planning and enjoying a meal with some friends. As you make a reservation, you consult your memory of past outings. What has worked before and what hasn't? What makes most sense for this occasion, given what you've learned? Memory serves as a backdrop for present experience.

The second part of prudence is **understanding**. This kind of understanding is something other than the virtue of the speculative intellect we described earlier. This understanding concerns knowledge of the present. Specifically, it is the part of prudence that instantaneously sizes up a particular action. By understanding, you have a sense for whether or not this is *to be done* before ever making a judgment. You still need to reason upon the proposed action, but understanding provides an initial evaluation of the task. You preview a particular action and have a feel for how it ought to go.

In time with the Lord, there is opportunity to revisit the past, ask for insight, and think through connections, and then anticipate how you might respond again in similar circumstances.

Again, when planning the evening out, you might have the intuitive sense that, given those in attendance, you ought to play it safe. Adventurous dining can be fun, but this group is just getting comfortable with each other. So too, in the course of the meal, you might "see" what needs to be said or done in order to draw everyone into the conversation and out of themselves.

The third part of prudence is **docility**. In general, there are two ways of acquiring knowledge. Either you can learn it on your own (by discovery) or from another (by instruction). Docility aids with receiving instruction. For any number of reasons, you might find it difficult to consult others about decisions. Perhaps it's laziness. Perhaps it's pride. As a result, you might not perceive the benefit of docility in decision making. And yet, practical matters are so various that there's no way to consider every avenue well in a reasonable amount of time. From this vantage, it's a great help to have the assistance of those who are older or wiser. Their experience and their prudent reasoning may be of great service. But, to access this font of wisdom, we have to humble ourselves and ask for it. We have to love the truth more than we love ourselves. Docility means a genuine open-mindedness. As Josef Pieper writes in *The Four Cardinal Virtues*, "What is meant [by docility] is the ability to take advice, sprung not from any vague 'modesty,' but simply from the desire for real understanding."

To be docile, you have to overcome obstacles to seeking counsel, remain open to what is offered, and then weigh and incorporate that input. This doesn't mean that you should become hesitant, impressionable, or enslaved to others' pronouncements. To be prudent means to be genuinely self-actualized, albeit with the recognition that there is much to be gained from the counsel of others. "Trust in the LORD with all your heart, / and do not rely on your own insight" (Prv 3:5). "Stand in the assembly of the elders. Who is wise? Cleave to him" (Sir 6:34).

Returning to the evening's events — it can help to consult some reviews and food critics ahead of time. Perhaps you'll learn that the restaurant operates by European standards of hospitality and that, if you're going to get the check, you'll have to ask for it directly. Seeking advice saves you from some awkward indecision at the end of the meal.

The fourth part of prudence is **shrewdness**, sometimes called sagacity or acumen. Whereas docility aids with instruction, shrewdness aids with discovery. Shrewdness is a keen first estimate or judgment of what should be done. By comparison to understanding, which intuits the situation, shrewdness assesses it. The shrewd person has a knack for settling practical matters. He or she works them out effortlessly by a kind of nimbleness of mind, always at the ready with very reliable snap judgments.

The importance of shrewdness reveals something significant about prudence. The practical wisdom that prudence provides isn't necessarily a matter of lengthy deliberation. It may be worthwhile to consider a course of action for a period of time, but prudence comes from the quality, not the quantity, of that consideration. It doesn't really matter if you've thought a lot about it. It matters that you've thought well about it. The goodness of an action is measured by its being done virtuously. When the Lord called the first of the apostles, the Gospel recounts, "And immediately they left their nets and followed him" (Mk 1:18). Was that hasty of them? Might they have taken some time to think it through? In this case, they didn't need to. They had been awaiting the Lord, and they recognized him when he arrived. Theirs was a genuinely excellent response to a genuinely excellent call. By shrewdness, they judged in an instant, and by prudence they responded with the assent of their whole person.

Back at the restaurant, you draw upon shrewdness to coordinate the order. After quite a few minutes, everyone continues perusing the menu non-committally despite the waiter's increasing impatience. At an opportune moment, you gently but firmly settle on a couple bottles of wine for the table and foster consensus for hors d'oeuvres, helping all present to arrive at a choice with which they are pleased.

The fifth part of prudence is **reasoning**, used here to signify the way that the human intellect moves step by step when working out a choice. As human beings, we are made toward the goal of life, but we aren't quite there. To arrive at happiness, we must take the right steps. Our intellectual nature reflects this fact and reasoning sees to it that we take those steps well. We are intellectual pilgrims on a journey toward the goal, and part of being prudent is proceeding well along this pilgrimage of many movements.

Reasoning is especially visible in how you plan the evening. From start to finish, you see to every detail. You do the research and make the reservation. You alert the restaurant to your friends' dietary restrictions. You scout out parking, estimate transit time, and make sure each of your friends has all the information he or she needs. All is accounted for.

These first five integral parts — memory, understanding, docility, shrewdness, and reasoning — perfect prudence's work of knowing. The remaining three integral parts perfect prudence's work of commanding.

The sixth integral part of prudence is **foresight**. Foresight provides for the future by ensuring that we hold the end in mind when carrying out the action. In the moment, it can be easy to get a bit caught up, and at times, we risk losing ourselves in the excitement. Foresight has one look to the end. It's a kind of prudential recollection in the purpose of action.

The goal of your dinner is to enjoy the company of some old friends and make some new ones. When one friend alerts you that she'll be late in arriving, you are justly upset but take a moment to work out a solution. You could confront her for being irresponsible, but that's likely to dampen the mood and ruin the evening. So, you just have her meet you at the restaurant, not letting a little hiccup get in the way of the evening's enjoyment. Here, foresight holds the end in mind and sees to it that the action responds to that vision.

The seventh integral part of prudence is **circumspection**. Circumspection continues to compare the means to the end in the performance of the act. For instance, having arrived at the restaurant, your intention to enjoy a delicious meal looks a particular way at the outset. After you have eaten a bit or had a few drinks over the course of the evening, though, your thinking shifts on what that enjoyment entails. When you perceive that you may be expected to eat quite a lot in the circumstances, you begin splitting plates and leaving courses unfinished. When you realize that your friends are able to handle more than you, you start sipping a little slower and staggering your drink orders. As the act unfolds, it requires revisiting, and circumspection sees to that. If one were to simply sit down and say, "I am here to eat and drink" without ever revisiting the choice during the course of the evening, it might make for an uncomfortable and regrettable meal.

The eighth and final integral part of prudence is **caution**. Caution avoids obstacles that appear in the performance of an action. With many good choices, some potentially perilous circumstances may be mixed in. That's just the way of contingent and complex realities. Caution gauges these circumstances in order to avoid or manage them. For instance, you know that certain topics may come up in the course of the evening, and if they do, the conversation may be a bit tense. You prepare in anticipation and remain on the lookout as the meal progresses. Mindful of your friends' sensitivities and strongly held opinions, you're able to facilitate an engaging discussion and chart a course around any potential pitfalls.

Interestingly enough, when many people think of prudence, they only think of caution. Remember that popular appraisal of prudence at the end of the last chapter? It sounded a lot like what we just identified as caution, one of eight integral parts. Caution is part of the story, but it's not the whole story. If we treat it as the whole story, we end up with a limited understanding of prudence. We can't content ourselves with that. We want the full grandeur of prudence.

Clearly, prudence is an amazing virtue bringing a tremendous variety of resources to bear on human action. All at once, prudence helps mine the past, build the present, and secure the future. It weighs past experience, draws from the wisdom of others, perfects our instincts, refines our judgments, disciplines our thinking, looks down the road, anticipates the unforeseen, and improvises when necessary.

Caution is part of the story, but it's not the whole story. If we treat it as the whole story, we end up with a limited understanding of prudence.

Prudence is the virtue that perfects practical reason in all of its ins and outs. It's an excellence *for the way*, suiting us beautifully to a life *on the way*.

Reflect

Given that the goal of the virtue of prudence is essentially practical, what is the benefit of understanding all these detailed philosophical distinctions? How do the different stages of human action and acts of prudence help you to make sense of your life and choose confidently?

Is the priority of command reflected in your own approach to life, or do you sometimes get stuck in analysis paralysis? Now that you grasp the reality that counsel looks to judgment, and judgment looks to command, do you need to (or how might you) adjust your approach to everyday choices?

Which of the eight integral parts of prudence come as a surprise to you? What place do these perfections occupy in your present approach to making decisions? What place might they occupy in a future approach?

5

Am I Whole?

In the previous chapter, we took prudence apart to examine its different acts and parts. There our discussion worked like a mechanic disassembling an engine into component parts. In this chapter, we'll take the opposite approach. With the work of breaking down behind us, it's time for building up. Here the discussion will work like a mechanic assembling a car, starting from the chassis, suspension, transmission, and engine. We will situate prudence in the context of the whole moral life to show how it "drives" that whole. *Whole*, here, means something that is integrated or unified. For a human person, to be whole is to live coherently or consistently for a meaningful purpose. Prudence brings about this wholeness by conducting us steadily to the goal of human flourishing.

The Virtues Are Connected

Not unlike the parts of a car, which are manufactured for assembly, so too, the virtues are designed to fit and work together. Saint Ambrose writes, "The virtues are connected and linked together, so that whoever has one, is seen to have several." Saint Augustine adds, "The virtues that reside in the human mind are quite inseparable from one another." Their observations square with our experience. Where one virtue is seen, more are sure to be found. If I see that a coworker is kind and objective in a conflict, I can safely assume that she's also peaceable and forgiving. Every once in a while you'll find exceptions, but virtuous people tend to be virtuous throughout. The virtues, it turns out, are connected. By the same token, the vices, too, are connected. Cicero writes, "If you confess to not having one particular virtue, it must needs be that you have none at all." Saint Gregory adds, "One virtue without the other is either of no account whatever, or very imperfect." If I see pride or vainglory in a man, I'm not surprised to learn later that he is easily offended and dishonest. Persons with grave moral faults often have a whole host of vices crowding around inside them, and they're likely to breed more.

This connection among the virtues isn't accidental or haphazard. It's part of the design. If one is temperate, he or she doesn't just *happen* to be prudent, just, and courageous. In reality, the virtues actually reinforce each other. They encourage, inspire, or even cause each other to grow and to flourish. Most of this chapter describes how prudence causes the moral virtues. It's also true, though, that the moral virtues cause prudence, albeit in a different way. Aristotle has a shorthand way for capturing this phenomenon. He says, "As the man is, so he sees." So, if a man is good or virtuous, then he will reason well or virtuously. In other words, if a man is just, courageous, and temperate, then he will be prudent as well. For, if he has the moral virtues, his well-formed desires aid him to have well-formed thoughts.

Aristotle describes why this is so. He explains that, in practical things, the ends of the moral virtues each work like principles. Principles here mean something like points of departure. They are what motivate or give rise to action. The end of justice is simply what is due to the other. The end of fortitude is difficult sense goods and evils. The end of temperance is simple sense goods and evils. Concretely speaking, these ends may be as humble as satisfying hunger (temperance) or as lofty as worshiping God (justice). Regardless of whether they are low or high, though, a virtuous person develops an orderly appetite for these ends or an orderly relationship to them. He learns to love them well and within bounds. This then affects how he thinks about them — a virtuous person is more likely to think about ends well when it comes to making decisions. He is better disposed to be prudent.

To illustrate this point, say you're headed down the block to have a much-anticipated lunch at a local diner. As you walk along, you recall that you owe $10 to a friend. As it turns out, you only have $10 on you. Then, as luck would have it, you see this friend standing in front of the diner in conversation with a police officer. From a distance, you hear the police officer say, "You can't just leave your flashers on. You have to pay the $10 parking." You also happen to know that your friend is overwhelmed by responsibilities right now and strapped for cash. If anyone is deserving of your aid, it's her. Because you are just, courageous, and temperate, you see the meeting as providential and your arrival as timely. Here is an opportunity to repay a debt and lend a hand. You don't think for a minute about how you'll miss out on lunch. It doesn't even occur to you. And so, disposed as you are to act prudently, you hurry over to your friend, pay the parking cost, and maybe even extend a dinner invitation for later in the week. Because you have orderly appetites, you see the situation well, more or less, and so act prudently.

Aristotle goes on to explain that the inverse is equally true. If you are the slave of malformed appetites, you will see poorly. Injustice, cowardice, and intemperance each dispose to imprudence. The man who is consumed by a life of vice neither loves nor pursues the ends of the moral virtues as he should; and since he desires perversely, his view of reality is skewed. He sees exclusively in the selfish terms of satisfying his needs. Failings in justice, fortitude, and temperance dispose him to failings in prudence.

Return to the diner, but this time from a vicious perspective. Again, you notice your friend out front in conversation with a police officer. This time, though, you hesitate. At this point in your day, the thought of returning home and preparing a turkey sandwich is just too much to handle. People are always asking you to make sacrifices, but every now and then you need to spend a little something on yourself. After all, your $10 isn't the only $10 that your friend could use to pay for parking. Technically, you never said when you'd pay her back. What's another few days? With these thoughts in mind, you sneak in the side entrance to the diner and leave your friend to her fate. This is imprudent, given your motives, but it's not surprising. You were disposed to imprudence by an inability to recognize what is due to another (injustice), an unwillingness to labor in the kitchen (cowardice), and an inordinate attachment to diner food (intemperance). Behold the flip side of the coin. "As the man is, so he sees."

black + white

don't see in rationality

From this illustration, it's evident that we need the moral virtues to be truly prudent. Without them, we flounder. From one vantage, this can be dispiriting, especially given our moral weakness. Seen from another perspective, though, it can be encouraging. Moral virtue is a force multiplier: Growth in moral virtue means growth in prudence, growth in one's whole moral life. The moral virtues heal and elevate desire, and in so doing, they clarify our thinking and dispose us to prudent action. As we become better, we see better. As we grow in moral virtue, we grow in prudence. But while the moral virtues cause prudence, prudence also causes the

The moral virtues heal and elevate desire, and in so doing, they clarify our thinking and dispose us to prudent action.

moral virtues in its own way. It's to this aspect that we now turn.

The Charioteer of the Virtues

When describing the cardinal virtues, St. Bernard of Clairvaux refers to prudence as the "charioteer of the virtues." According to the image, the charioteer (prudence) sets out with a purpose in mind, namely, winning the race. To that end, he drives his horses (justice, fortitude, and temperance), spurring them on and reining them in, as need be. If he is to compete well, the charioteer must know his horses and how best to treat them. He must also know how they interact with each other so he can coordinate their movements. Effectively, the charioteer is responsible for integrating and unifying his team in pursuit of victory.

From this image, we get a basic understanding of how prudence directs the moral virtues and so makes the human person whole. First, prudence oversees the movements of the individual virtues. Each virtue has its own particular end and inclination: Justice concerns what is due to the other; fortitude concerns difficult sense goods; temperance concerns simple sense goods. Prudence, like a charioteer who knows his horses, gets to know these different inclinations and identifies the best ways to achieve them. Prudence drives each of the lower virtues to its fullest potential by alternately spurring them on and reining them in as it presses on toward victory.

Second, since it has the power to see the whole of life, prudence draws together the movements of the moral virtues and drives them to its own overarching end. In effect, prudence trains the moral virtues into a team. Like the charioteer who might place the strong, impetuous horse in the front and the calm, veteran horse mid-pack, prudence coordinates the moral virtues so as to get the most out of each. In the process, it also raises them to a higher pursuit. Left to themselves, horses don't dream of winning a race. It's the charioteer who dreams of such feats. If they succeed, though, both charioteer and horses share in the same victory. Likewise, justice, fortitude, and temperance don't think in terms of the whole of life. Prudence, though, thinks for them. Prudence holds the goal in mind as it spurs the moral virtues on toward the victory of integral and unified human flourishing under the rule of faith and reason, carried on by the inspiration of the Holy Spirit. To appreciate better how prudence causes the moral virtues, let's look closer at these two main features of prudence's whole-making work.

Inclinations and the Natural Law

The first dimension of prudence's whole-making work is to help the individual moral virtues achieve their ends. Prudence, the charioteer, tends the stable of the moral virtues by sizing up their different pursuits and identifying the best ways to go about them. In this work, prudence deals with the different *inclinations* of each of the moral virtues. Inclinations describe the different ways we tend toward different ends, whether those be food, drink, family life, or divine worship. The moral virtues train and perfect these inclinations. In fact, a moral virtue is effectively a healed and elevated inclination for some human end. Prudence helps the moral virtues along by establishing order in these different inclinations. Since inclinations are so foundational for grasping this concept, we will spend a moment trying to better understand their significance.

From a cursory look at creation, we can see that every creature gravitates spontaneously toward what makes it whole. Plants send out roots to collect both water and nutrients and turn their leaves toward the sun's rays. Animals flee from predators and care for their young in order to fill out their flock, pack, or herd. Human beings plant crops, husband animals, build cities, and seek to know truths of the highest order. Each creature seeks the fulfillment of its nature in the way it "knows" best.

In the case of our own human nature, there are certain basic inclinations that define who we are and how we are meant to be. First, we want to keep on being. And so, we are naturally inclined to stay in existence. Second, we want to ensure the survival of our species. And so, we are naturally inclined to family life. Third, we want to cultivate meaningful relationships. And so, we are naturally inclined to know the truth about God and to live peaceably in society.

These inclinations (among others) aren't just something tacked onto our nature as an afterthought. They are at the heart of what it means for us to be human, so deeply impressed in our natures that we refer to them as a law — the natural law. To say that the inclinations are a law means that, if we are to flourish, we must follow them. That doesn't suggest that we can just abandon ourselves to them. Our inclinations, especially those most basic inclinations to food, drink, and sexual intercourse, are often disorderly. This comes as no surprise since they flow from fallen powers of a fallen nature. As we saw earlier, we experience ignorance in the intellect, malice in the will, and a combination of weakness and concupiscence in the passions. As a result, our natural and good inclinations cannot always be relied upon to track consistently with the true good. Even though we may recognize that a higher good (like the worship of God offered at Sunday Mass) should be preferred to a lower good (like eight hours of sleep after a late night), it may still be hard to choose the higher good when the lower good is very attractive. How, then, do we heal and elevate these different inclinations? How do we follow the natural law? By growth in moral virtue. The moral virtues clarify the natural law for us and empower us to carry it out. They free us for excellence and direct us toward happiness.

Ends and Means

In the work of healing and elevating these inclinations, prudence occupies a special place. It exercises a kind of leadership by forming an estimation of the ends of the moral virtues and identifying the best means to those ends. Prudence, the charioteer, trains each of the moral virtues for the roles they are to play in the race and drives them on to the attainment of true human excellence.

The human person is presented with a variety of good ends in need of ordering. Some rank higher while others rank lower, and a choice of one may exclude the choice of another. At a glance, the prudent person is able to take in all these goods, comprehend them, and fix each in its place. Prudence is able to do so because it can survey the whole landscape of human pursuits. It's not limited to just this or that good. It accounts for everything that is properly human.

To master a language, you can't just focus on grammar or vocabulary or listening or speaking to the exclusion of other dimensions. It all has to be taken together to become truly proficient. Prudence helps you to master the language of the whole of human life. It's the virtue of human fluency. Aristotle writes that the prudent man is "able to deliberate well about what is good and expedient for himself, not in some particular respect, e.g. about what sorts of things conduce to health or to strength, but about what sorts of things conduce to the good life in general." While other virtues are determined to some specific domain of human activity, prudence is focused on human totality. From this standpoint, the prudent person esteems different goods as they ought to be esteemed — according to the role they play in genuine human flourishing.

Because of the overarching perspective that prudence enjoys, it can help the moral virtues to size up their ends, to identify means, and to perfect inclinations along the way. Each moral virtue has its own proper excellence. The virtue of justice heals and elevates the will, rectifying one's relationships by rendering to the other what is due. The virtue of fortitude heals and elevates the passions by steeling one against difficulties — alternately urging on to confrontation and cautioning from recklessness. The virtue of temperance heals and elevates the passions for food and drink and sexual intercourse (in the setting of married life) by heartening one to enjoy these goods while retaining sobriety of spirit. Left to themselves, these virtues have a sense for their proper excellence, but they don't necessarily know how to go about selecting means to those ends. This is the task of prudence, because only prudence, informed by law and grace, knows what acting reasonably looks like in the circumstances.

The ends of the moral virtues, we have seen, are just part of the natural law. The human person is built to desire preservation of existence, family life, and genuine communion. The moral virtues don't have to discover their ends. They are provided by human nature. However, the means to those ends have to be discerned by reason, and the moral virtues are not, of themselves, reasonable. The moral virtues live in the appetites — the will and the passions. They don't live in the intellect. Thus, they need a reasonable virtue — prudence — to help them sort out the means to their naturally-given ends.

Prudence is responsible for determining *how*: *how* to be just, *how* to be courageous, and *how* to be temperate.

Prudence is responsible for determining *how*: *how* to be just, *how* to be courageous, and *how* to be temperate. In the case of justice, prudence grasps when to punish or to pardon in light of the common good. In the case of fortitude, prudence discerns concretely whether to fight, to flee, or to endure, given the persons involved. In the case of temperance, prudence supplies the particular insight into what's too much or too little given the time and the place. The moral virtues form the appetites to desire well, while prudence applies the reason to think well. Prudence chooses among different desires, directing one in the concrete choice between a corporate reimbursement or a personal expenditure, between a pull-up jump shot or a drive to the hoop, between two cocktails or three. Prudence sizes up the different goods at stake and then selects the best means for achieving the ends.

Coordinating the Virtues

The second dimension of prudence's whole-making work is intimately associated with the first dimension. Prudence, the charioteer, coordinates the movements of the moral virtues and drives them together toward its goal. Prudence assembles and harnesses its team to fashion an integrated and unified life bent on human flourishing.

Let's return briefly to the discussion of inclinations. The moral virtues each have inclinations to their respective ends: Justice is inclined to what is due to the other, fortitude to difficult sense goods and evils, and temperance to simple sense goods and evils. It's not only the moral virtues that have inclinations, though. Prudence has its own inclination as well, an inclination not of appetite but of thought. Aristotle writes, "All men, by nature, desire to know." As we have said, sometimes that knowledge is for knowing's sake, and sometimes it is for doing's sake. Prudence guides this latter inclination to the practical truth, moving us to choose well for what makes us flourish. In effect, prudence heals and elevates the inclination of practical reason — the reason's pursuit of what is to be done, and not just in this or that setting, but for the whole of life.

While it holds this truth in mind, prudence calls upon the moral force of justice, fortitude, and temperance for achieving the end that it alone is able to understand. In the process, the moral virtues come to their most excellent expression in the fulfillment of the whole. With prudence driving them onward, the rigor of justice, the audacity of fortitude, and the moderation of temperance all assume their highest realization. How does this play out in the concrete? Let's say that you are, by temperament, a very anxious and detail-oriented person. Often, your mind is consumed with practical things, especially when those things seem urgent. You are trying to manage it but only with limited success. Unsurprisingly, this disposition makes it hard for you to pray. You try to meditate for thirty minutes each morning, but your mind wanders toward practical things. When this happens, you set aside your prayer in order to list your action items. You muse to yourself that, perhaps, this is what the Lord wanted you to pray about. If you're honest, though, you don't really believe the rationalization. For, although momentarily relieved by re-hearsing the day's duties, you soon feel disappointed that you were so easily deflected from your prayer.

As of late, however, you have had some successes. On a couple of occasions, you were able to resist the urge and persevere in your meditation. When that happened, your mind was soon quieted as you attended to the Lord less anxiously. As you have grown in virtue, prudence inte-riorizes the experience of these successes and calls upon the pertinent virtues to aid you when the occasion next arises. As the mental list begins to populate, prudence kin-dles justice to recall that your commitment to the worship of God is more important than these little tasks. Further, prudence commands fortitude to quell the fear that what is not immediately written down will necessarily be for-gotten. It also tasks temperance the night before to ensure a good night's sleep, apart from which this prayer time wouldn't have been possible in the first place. In this one simple act, justice, fortitude, and temperance are all drawn into worship through the coordination of prudence. Each of the moral virtues participate in the victory of prayer, and, in the act, your moral life comes together in the pur-suit of a wholly human end.

Prudence, Saint Thomas teaches, is like the provi-dence of the moral virtues. Just as providence disposes creatures sweetly and strongly within a well-orchestrated divine plan, so prudence draws the moral virtues into its own rational designs. Prudence is able to account well for the whole course of our human lives. Whereas the moral virtues lower their eyes and plow ahead, prudence stands upright and surveys the scene as it sets about its wise work. By taking into account the whole of the human affair, prudence gives full scope to justice, fortitude, and temperance, looking beyond their blinders into its own plenary vision.

Which leads us back to the image of prudence as charioteer of the virtues. Prudence, we have seen, is uniquely suited to assist the moral virtues in their respective pursuits and draw them into a wholly human work. Apart from prudence, they may exhibit some excellence or achieve certain goods, but they will never reach their full potential. The moral virtues without prudence are like untrained horses. When they're running wild or resisting the breaker's whip, they may be inspiring, but they're also terrifying — beautiful at a distance, but scary up close. Once trained though, these horses become part of a human work — employable for labor and leisure alike, called into genuine human pursuits. It's from among their ranks that you have your war horses and race horses, the great horses of memory. Under the tutelage of the trainer, the cavalryman, and the jockey, these horses do something special. So too with the moral virtues. Under the care of prudence, the charioteer of the virtues, the moral virtues are driven to the realization of their ends and coordinated in the work of human flourishing.

Infusing Reason

By distilling the insights taken from the charioteer images, we can think of prudence as the reason of the virtuous appetites. Prudence, in its interaction with the will and passions, can be said to *infuse* reason into every aspect of human life. From beyond the bounds of the intellect, prudence's insight into the practical truth overflows into the appetites, inspiring virtuous action and shaping the appetites accordingly. This can be seen in two main ways.

First, prudence infuses the appetites with a habitual desire for a reasonable life. Aristotle writes that the moral virtues direct the appetites to a kind of mean, maneuvering them between excess or defect. The courageous man, for instance, wends his way between rashness (excess) and cowardice (defect) and the temperate man navigates between overindulgence (excess) and insensibility (defect). This mean is determined by prudence, but the determination actually spills into the very appetite itself. To give an everyday example, think of your approach to the kids' menu. At a certain point, we all stop ordering from it. That first departure may be a conscious decision to set aside childish things, but at a certain point, we just move on from it entirely. Imagine going back to the kids' menu now. Chances are that we no longer even enjoy those meals. Our appetites have changed. We want food that is more substantial and real. What is true of food is also true of the good more generally. As prudence infuses reason into our appetites over the years, we come in time to desire what is more substantial and real in human life.

Second, the appetites themselves come to interact more reasonably. One of the effects of the wounds of original sin is that we enter the world in an unreasonable state.

Each of our appetites seeks its end with little concern for how it ought to coordinate with the others. Each appetite acts like a pouty child endlessly repeating "Mine!" Before the fall, man would have found it easy to pursue a variety of human goods in orderly fashion. Now, it is exceedingly difficult. By infusing reason into the appetites, though, prudence begins to order the appetites according to the pattern of their original harmony. Each appetite is empowered to interact fruitfully and reasonably with the others, because each has been made part of reason's integral and unified work. The whole of one's life has been made to bear the mark of reason.

Both of these aspects of infusing reason involve the moral virtues. Moral virtues mature the appetites and help to coordinate a reasonable harmony among them. St. Thomas Aquinas writes that "Moral virtue is a habit accompanied by right reason, which, of course, is prudence." The moral virtues, as the allies of prudence, work with reason to reintegrate and unify the human person. As a result, the moral virtues come to share in the nobility of prudence's dignity. The moral virtues experience something of prudence's providence. To illustrate this, take the example of temperance.

Left to itself, temperance just concerns food, drink, and sexual intercourse. There's nothing about its activity, though, that is distinctively human. We share its inclinations with cows and kangaroos. But, when taken up by prudence, temperance goes well beyond the animal kingdom. As Josef Pieper writes: "Only by means of this

perfected ability to make good choices [prudence] are in-
stinctive inclinations toward goodness [appetites] exalted
into the spiritual core of man's decisions, from which truly
human acts arise." In alliance with prudence, temperance
is drawn more fully into the life of reason. In this setting,
whether one is selecting the menu for a dinner party or
deciding to fast on Wednesdays and Fridays, the choice
takes on a new aspect. The passions are still engaged, but
as suffused with reason's judgment.

Temperance, here, isn't just a matter of slowing down
and saying no. Prudence draws it into a richer human story, one that prudence alone is able to tell. For the temperate
woman, it is not enough to say, "I am inclined to family
life, therefore I will marry this man standing next to me
and begin." That might not be the best choice, especially if
the particular man under consideration is very young or is
about to leave the country for a work rotation or is called
to a religious vocation. In the end, the human person is
ordered to a whole life, a life of integrity and unity, one
in which the moral virtues play an important role — one
perfected and coordinated by the virtue of prudence.

Prudence, with its infusion of reason, is simply the
human excellence *par excellence*. It's the competence that
sorts out the different aspects of one's life and brings them
together in the pursuit of happiness. It's in this spirit that
the Desert Fathers refer to prudence as "the mother, the
guardian, and the director of the virtues." Prudence gathers the power of the lower virtues, spurs them on according to its clear-sighted vision, and guides each in its proper

place. Prudence sees to the perfection of a whole person, for it is the place of prudence to integrate, to unify, and ultimately to infuse the whole of human life with its reasonable excellence.

Reflect

Are there particular virtues you feel like you need to work on? How might growth in those virtues help with growth in prudence?

What are some practical steps you can take toward establishing a more prudent prayer life?

Think of some moments in your day where you feel overwhelmed by desire, whether to eat a snack or look at your phone or something else. What role does your conscious thought ordinarily play at those times? How can prudence infuse reason into those moments?

6

Am I Bold?

Thought only gets us so far. Eventually, thought has to be translated into action. It's good to be thoughtful, but it's better yet to be bold. Prudence is the virtue responsible for translating thought into action, and the prudent person is a man or woman of action. Unfortunately, though, this aspect of prudence tends to be diminished by many Christians, and instead of a healthy emphasis on acting or doing, there arises an unhealthy emphasis on pondering or discerning.

Part of the reason for this is that, in both theory and practice, prudence is often edged out by conscience. Instead of stressing prudence, we stress conscience. Conscience, though, is not nearly so bold as prudence. Prudence is immediately and directly practical. Conscience is not. How then do we address the current imbalance? First, we'll study conscience to determine its rightful place in the moral life. Then, we'll turn to prudence to see how it differs from conscience. Finally, we'll conclude with a comparison of the two. As we'll see, conscience evaluates, whereas prudence both evaluates and acts. By reaffirming the rightful place of prudence, perhaps we can recover something of the boldness of the moral life that is often lost from view.

What Is Conscience?

Whether we are making decisions or evaluating their morality, we often speak in terms of conscience. How do I form my conscience? How do I know what my conscience is telling me? Can I really be confident in following my conscience? In practical matters, conscience helps to facilitate our moral reasoning. It gets some principles on the table, applies them to particular situations, and works toward resolutions. All of that, though, sounds a lot like how we have described prudence. What, then, is conscience, and how does it differ from prudence?

St. Thomas Aquinas teaches that conscience is neither a power of the soul (like the intellect, will, or passions) nor a virtue (like faith, wisdom, prudence, or justice). Rather, conscience is an *act* of the intellect. It's part of how we think about our human lives and choices. In general, it concerns the same types of things that prudence concerns — human acts and their morality. Conscience differs from prudence, though, in how it treats those things. Prudence directly concerns action. It performs the act under consideration. Conscience, by contrast, indirectly concerns action. It assesses the act under consideration. The dictate of conscience may be carried out eventually, but it is primarily and principally about evaluation.

Effectively, conscience is a tool for appropriating the moral law — for making the moral law one's own. The moral law exists, whether one acknowledges it or not. If one seeks to live well within its bounds, though, he or she has to appropriate it by acquiring moral knowledge. What exactly does this look like? As man comes of age, he fashions a rough and ready reserve of moral knowledge — his current sense of the moral law. Over the course of a lifetime, he refines this moral knowledge so that it accounts better for his experience. Conscience facilitates this growth by sizing up particular acts against what he currently knows and giving feedback.

In this task, conscience evaluates the goodness of both past and future moral actions. If it's a future deed that one is contemplating, then conscience may instigate, encourage, caution, or bind. "You really ought to consider this," conscience might advocate. If it's a past deed that one is revisiting, then conscience defends, excuses, accuses, or nags. "You really ought to apologize," conscience might suggest. Ultimately, judgments of conscience help one to come into more perfect possession of moral knowledge. Within its domain, conscience is an invaluable tool for appropriating the moral law.

Conscience and the Natural Law

Conscience makes its judgments based upon two sources of practical truth. The first source is the moral knowledge that one acquires throughout the course of his or her life. The second and more basic source is the natural law. In the last chapter we described how the natural law works through human inclinations, prompting and guiding the pursuit of different goods. In addition to working through inclinations, though, the natural law also works through thought. The natural law can be known, and human beings can reason on the basis of it.

All human beings recognize the natural law to a certain extent, and there is pretty significant agreement on the fundamentals of what's good and what's evil. Respect for elders, good. Murder of innocent, evil. There may be some dispute over the details, but that shouldn't distract from the considerable consensus. From a Christian perspective, we know that this consensus isn't accidental or random, nor is it likely to change. It's part of who we are. We are capable of genuine insight into moral realities because that insight flows from our very nature given by God. The light of the intellect, our sharing in the divine light, reveals to us a vast and intelligible moral universe. By our intellectual capacity to access the very natures of things, we are empowered to know who we are and how we ought to engage with our environment. The natural law gives us an habitual "sense" for the law of God inscribed in us at creation. Since it is part of our nature, the natural law cannot be blotted out. It is a permanent feature of human life. It may be obscured and our sensitivity to it deadened, but it always remains. It is an ineradicable consequence of our being made in the image of God.

This habit of the natural law illustrates how our life ought to look in its most basic contours. When stated in such terms, though, it may seem a bit abstract. How, then, is the natural law brought to bear on human life in real time? From the light of the mind, the natural law gives rise to certain principles by which to live. The most foundational of these is "Do good and avoid evil." From this starting point, we can tease out further principles like "Honor your father and mother" or "Thou shalt not kill." These principles, and those that flow from them, begin to give concrete shape to our life of practical reason.

These basic principles don't give us enough detail to evaluate particular acts though, so we need more refinement. The natural law has to be further determined and applied. With the principles at work in the background, we fashion more specific arrangements and laws concerning worship, politics, family life, human sexuality, properties and contracts, courtesy and social discourse, and so on. What do these determinations and applications look like? Take one example: In the state of Pennsylvania, car theft is punishable by up to seven years in prison and up to $15,000 in fines. At first blush, that law may seem somewhat arbitrary and far removed from the natural law, but on closer inspection there are good reasons for it.

We begin with the principle "Do good and avoid evil." Whatever policy is decided, it should promote integral human flourishing. Next, we have to acknowledge the place of private property. Man has the right to procure and dispense of private property within a responsible and peaceable society. If property rights are not safeguarded and theft condoned, we run the risk of lawless chaos. Further, when someone transgresses the law, justice has to be meted out in proportionate punishment which a) reflects the gravity of the crime, b) deters other would-be criminals, and c) reforms the criminal himself. Thus, given the value of security and civil order, the cost and importance of a car in modern life, and the relative weight of similar infractions, the legislature of Pennsylvania settled upon this law. It's not immediately obvious that it's the best possible arrangement, but the legislature was certainly reasonable in making it, for at root the determination arises from the natural law and applies it well. From the natural law, we eventually make our way to the nitty-gritty details of life, like car theft. It's on these grounds that Saint Thomas refers to the principles of the natural law as a kind of seed plot from which grows all of our subsequent practical reasoning. The natural law empowers us to seek what is good and to turn against what is evil in every dimension of our individual and social lives.

The Judgment of Conscience

From its grounding in natural law, the judgment of conscience makes concrete determinations and applications of moral knowledge. Judgments of conscience are formulated like arguments with premises and conclusions.

In a judgment of conscience: 1) the natural law supplies one premise; 2) moral knowledge concerning a particular action supplies the other premise; and 3) the act of conscience draws the conclusion from the premises. The conclusion is an application of moral knowledge concerning a particular action. It concretizes what is implicit in the premises by teasing out the implications of the natural law and moral knowledge.

Let's say that you have been working for three months in one of your company's foreign offices, and you have to get a driver's license in your new country of residence before the year is out. To get the license, you need to pass a theory exam. Now, you could study the 119-page manual written in a foreign language or you could just bring your phone to the licensing center and look up the answers discreetly and efficiently. The rules of the road don't differ much, and you probably wouldn't be endangering anyone. What does it matter if you don't know precisely how many centimeters you have to leave between your tire and the curb? In the judgment of conscience informing your decision, the argument plays out as follows:

1. The one premise is supplied by the natural law: "Evil is to be avoided." This is a basic intellectual inclination — the first principle of practical reason — to which everyone everywhere has access.

2. The other premise is supplied by one's moral knowledge of the particular act: "Cheating

on this driver's exam would be evil." Here you recognize that, even though it may seem harmless, it is still an instance of cheating and, thus, an act of injustice.

3. From these two premises, then, you judge: "One should avoid cheating on this driver's exam." The conclusion is the judgment of conscience — an application of moral knowledge.

In this particular judgment, you begin with a basic principle of the natural law: Evil is to be avoided. You don't reason to it. You just recognize it. It registers deep in your person, deeper than any stated rule or regulation. At the level of the natural law, everyone knows that evil diminishes our humanity, that it makes us less of a person and undermines human flourishing. Regardless of time, place, or person involved, evil is to be avoided because it is dehumanizing. That being said, though, the principle is not especially concrete, nor is it immediately evident how it applies in the current circumstances. Thus, you need another premise to facilitate that application. You move then to the level of the particular by considering the nature of the act under consideration. Throughout the course of your life, you have acquired moral knowledge, gaining better appreciation for what is good and evil, and for what is permissible and forbidden. Against the backdrop of your moral knowledge, you examine the particular act. In your country, culture, church, and home, cheating is frowned upon and discouraged. It merits punishment. It causes you to feel uneasy beforehand and guilty afterwards. From this vantage, animated by the natural law and motivated by your particular knowledge regarding this act, you then render a judgment as to whether or not it should be done.

And that's it. This should be done, or this should not be done. That's all that conscience offers. Conscience doesn't necessitate action of any sort. One can judge well what is right or wrong and still act against that judgment. You may subsequently choose to cheat on the theory exam. That wouldn't be a failing of conscience, though, because it's not conscience's responsibility. The work of conscience is effectively complete once it has refined or applied moral knowledge. It renders a judgment on a particular act and doesn't go further.

For instance, a man's conscience might judge correctly that he is engaged in a habitually sinful act, but that doesn't always mean — often doesn't mean — that he will change his behavior. The novelist Graham Greene knew quite well that his carryings-on were sinful and that they prevented him from receiving the sacraments. It's just that he preferred his carryings-on. Once, when visiting Italy with his mistress, Greene had the opportunity to meet Padre Pio, but turned it down. When asked why, he said, "I didn't want to change my life by meeting a saint, and I felt there was a good chance that he was one." Greene's choice illustrates that conscience may indicate, but it needn't motivate.

The point, here, isn't to criticize conscience for not

acting. It is simply to highlight conscience's limited scope. Conscience is not a virtue. It doesn't *make* you good. It doesn't make you *act* well. It evaluates the morality of an act in light of the natural law and applies moral knowledge to particular actions, but it consists in thought alone. There's no guarantee of action with conscience. For action, we need prudence.

The Judgment of Prudence

The judgment of prudence goes beyond thought alone. It applies thought to appetite, which is to say, it translates thought into the movement of the will and passions. Whereas the judgment of conscience has no immediate bearing on the practical order, the judgment of prudence does. It is always and everywhere ordered to action.

In a judgment of prudence, one employs a similar form of reasoning as in a judgment of conscience: The one premise is supplied by the natural law and the other premise is supplied by moral knowledge concerning a particular action. Take again the example of cheating, now as a judgment of prudence.

1. The one premise reads the same: "Evil is to be avoided."
2. The other premise reads the same as well: "Cheating on this driver's exam would be evil."
3. In the judgment of prudence, the conclusion is the actual act, the embodied choice of both

intellect and will not to do as tempted: "I will not cheat."

Recall that, in the judgment of conscience, the conclusion was "One should avoid cheating on this driver's exam." However, the judgment of prudence draws a different conclusion. But if the premises are the same, how do we account for that? Here is where prudence's relationship to appetite comes into play. At every step of the judgment of prudence, the intellect is in conversation with the will and the passions. As prudence carries out its judgment, it sees to it that right thinking is applied to right desiring. In this, it goes beyond the territory of mere "should" and "should not" and into the territory of "am doing" and "am not doing." For prudence to be truly prudence, it is not enough to know what is good; it must also *do* what is good. Thus, we can observe a twofold activity in the judgment of prudence. First, prudence applies general principles to particular situations, an application that it shares with conscience. Second, prudence applies those general principles to concrete works, an application that goes beyond conscience. The first application determines that cheating is to be avoided. The second application determines that you won't cheat.

The key is the coordination of intellect and appetite. Left to itself, the intellect lacks the wherewithal to perform an embodied act. It can only give indication as to what should and shouldn't be done. But, in association with the appetites, the intellect (guided by prudence) motivates a fuller response. This is not to say that the judgment of prudence is an act of the will. It's an act of the intellect, but one that immediately and directly informs the activity of the will and the passions and reflects their activity in turn. In the judgment of prudence, the intellect imbues the appetites with its reasons for acting, and the appetites move spontaneously to the good reasoned on by the intellect.

This is ultimately what distinguishes the judgment of prudence from the judgment of conscience. In terms of premises and conclusions, the two look almost identical, but the connection with appetite sets prudence apart from conscience as more immediately and directly practical. Conscience is like an armchair philosopher. It may have good ideas, but it will need some motivation to see those plans through. Prudence, by comparison, is like a politician who has the backing of financial resources and a competent staff. It has both good ideas and the means (or appetites) to bring them about. Prudence always reasons with an eye toward action. At every moment it holds in mind the successful realization of its intended purpose — the application of thought to appetite.

> **Conscience is like an armchair philosopher. It may have good ideas, but it will require some motivation to see those plans through.**

The Priority of Action

The connection between thought and appetite recalls prudence's distinctive excellence among the virtues. It is one thing to recognize the difference between good and evil; conscience does so, and man is better for it. Mere recognition isn't enough, though, if one aims to live coherently or consistently for a single, meaningful purpose. Genuine human flourishing requires one to choose for good and against evil and to persevere in that choice. This is another thing entirely. Prudence is poised for action of this sort. Prudence applies knowing to doing and engages one more fully in action. It takes one from mere recognition of what is good and what is evil to actually choosing good and avoiding evil. Prudence is a virtue. It *makes* one good, *makes* one act well. It forms good character.

Think again of the image of human life as a pilgrimage. Man lives his life *on the way.* He is en route to the eternal enjoyment of God, and he must grow in holiness to fit him for that end. In order to arrive, he has to take many steps in the life of grace. Of course, many of those steps are of a mental sort. Self-examination and contemplation, for instance, are both important dimensions of human growth. Still, though, they are not the whole of it. If the pilgrimage could all unfold within the borders of the mind, why did God bother to give man a body? Man is, by creation, a rational animal. To be human, then, means to embody thought — to translate thought to action. Thus, if man is to successfully wend his way to happiness by a journey of many steps, it will require him to apply thought to appetite. It will require him to act. It will require him to be prudent.

If man is to complete this pilgrimage, he can't set out

in aimless or disorderly fashion. A "just do it" mentality only works if the "it" is the right "it." He has to engage with the best of human goods, from God on down. Over the course of his life, he aims to get better at engaging these goods — to choose them ever more easily, promptly, and joyfully. In short, he aims to grow in virtue. The whole trajectory, though, is contingent upon a willingness to act, which willingness is the true face of prudence.

The hyper-cautious type isn't necessarily prudent. While there may be times to avoid risks, there are just as many times to take them. Is this grounds for thoughtless impetuousness, then? No. The point is not to act for acting's sake, but to act in response to a good, a good that may even require sacrifice. The prudent soldier isn't the one who flees from every fight so he can die another day. Were he to do so, he might lose his home, his country, and even his soul — a fate worse than death. The prudent soldier is the one who risks his life precisely when he must. Because he is willing to lose his life, he stands a chance of saving it and saving others. So, too, the prudent person is one who can identify opportunities for the good and seize them. If one envisions choice in this way, if one embodies the primacy of action, then life is filled with drama and excitement. Every deed matters, because every deed is part of shaping character and shaping destiny.

Every deed matters, because every deed is part of shaping character and shaping destiny.

Action and Penance

In the day-to-day, it is easy to overlook action and fixate on evaluation instead. When that happens, though, we end up missing out. If our moral imaginations are limited to what is permitted and forbidden, or we are less concerned with pursuing greatness and more concerned with remaining blameless, then we've got a problem. The point of the moral life isn't just to avoid sin. Were that so, the goal might as well be to die shortly after baptism. No, the point is to do good — to know, love, and serve the Lord, to undertake big, bold, and magnanimous things. Prudence sees to it that we respond to God's call and aim for genuine greatness.

If you take an action-centered approach, one informed by prudence, it's inevitable that you will make mistakes and commit sins. If you strive for the good, you will suffer misadventure. Fortunately, though, these day-to-day failures don't spell disaster. There is only one genuine tragedy in life, and that's not to become a saint. Truth be told, life isn't about never falling down; it's about pushing on and growing in virtue. Admittedly, that's hard, but God gives us the strength for it. At times, the emotional, psychological, and spiritual toll of falling feels heavy. In those moments, it is tempting to retreat into yourself and settle for sinlessness over saintliness. That temptation has to be resisted. You are made for bold action, not analysis paralysis. There's no salvation to be had in spinning your wheels thinking about sins and vices. Salvation is only to be had in living your life.

This is especially important in your preparation for and practice of the Sacrament of Confession. Obviously, moral evaluation is a big part of the Sacrament of Confession. An integral confession requires that you recount the sins you have committed — number and kind. Certainly, there is sin accounting to be done, but the sacrament isn't just about sin accounting. If it were, then every visit to the confessional would amount to an admission of failure, a clean slate, and not much more.

In addition to the pardon of sins, the sacrament also gives growth in holiness. When you confess your sins with contrition and receive absolution, you are empowered to be better and live better. It's more than a reset button. This should shape how you prepare for the sacrament. Of course, it's good to review the precepts of the Church, the Ten Commandments, and the seven deadly sins in one's examination. In addition, though, it's also good to revisit the virtues, gifts of the Holy Spirit, and the Beatitudes. How is God prompting you to grow? Where do you see his grace giving indication? How have you failed to respond to that, and how can you respond better? An examination like this better disposes you to receive the healing and elevating grace of the sacrament, to be a real actor in the sacrament, and to look toward the goal of God and salvation.

It can be easy to think of the priest (acting in the person of Christ) as the *real* actor in the sacrament, as if confession were just something done to the penitent. This isn't true, though. The priest is part of the sacrament, but not all of it. Granted, the priest confers absolution. That's huge. He may also have good insights and counsel. That's also helpful, but it's secondary. What's primary is that the penitent meets God in the sacrament, the God who gives grace to both heal from sin and grow in holiness. God acts to meet the penitent. The penitent acts in response to meet God. The priest acts to facilitate that encounter.

In the Sacrament of Penance, you aren't just getting done unto, you're doing as well. You contribute more than just attendance and regularity. You contribute yourself to the act. If done devoutly and perseveringly, it will make you good; it will make you act well. Admittedly, it's an especially punishing act at times. With each confession, you recognize candidly that you will be back before too long. Life is difficult, human nature is weak, and sin is seemingly unavoidable. Despite all that, though, virtue can be sought throughout. That's the goal. Through your use of the Sacrament of Confession, you can grow in virtue. Don't lose sight of that vision.

Substituting Evaluation for Action

If we lose sight of this vision, it's easy to grow anxious about our moral footing. You can envision how the lack of confidence takes hold in a person. Failing to rely upon the dynamism of prudence to secure growth and boldness, instead she frets over always having the "right" answer. Soon, she starts referring everything to the priest. She might seek his input just for clarification, at first. Then, she needs his counsel for reassurance. Finally, she is unable to act without it. In the process, emphasis shifts away from action in her virtuous life toward the evaluation of her moral standing. Whereas she may have formerly envisioned her moral life in terms of beatitude, grace, and virtue, soon she comes to speak only of conscience, obligation, and sin.

With this change, you can see how easy it becomes to live at a distance from the excitement of the moral life. For one thing, all moral evaluation now becomes the field of the expert. A focus on resolving moral problems gives the impression that the average believer is not competent to choose for herself in most cases. Practically every moral issue now seems too complicated to manage. Thus, they must always be brought to the priest. With this, though, one loses the boldness necessary to act, and the dynamism of a prudent life is all but lost.

This kind of approach simply doesn't equip one to live in the real world. In life, there are no invariable moral strategies. There is no life hack for flourishing. Action, in practical matters, must constantly be adapted to the unpredictability of changing circumstances. For that, rules are helpful, but they're not enough. One needs prudence. One must become a virtuoso of the moral life — prepared to improvise at a moment's notice. Past experience, helpful counsel, and keen insight give the prudent person what he needs to succeed in whatever challenge lies in store. You may make the right decision; you may make the wrong decision. Either way, you can learn and grow, with your action playing an instrumental role in your lifelong pursuit of the good. The person who thinks exclusively in terms of conscience, obligation, and sin is terrified at the prospect of failure, struggling to see her choices in terms of the big picture. Instead, she sees each crisis as an isolated instance for which she is ill-suited. What is needed in this setting isn't a technique, but a boldness suited to the complexity of life. What is needed is prudence.

Prudence is not an academic science reserved to the expert, nor is it an art to be wielded only by the skilled or advanced. Prudence is for everyone, forming each to engage an intricate world of moral realities and to do so well. This should mark our attitude toward the virtuous life. We are not primarily meant to memorize the finest of moral distinctions or master the rule book of life. Rather, we are meant to learn what is good and to grow each day in pursuit of it. Prudence makes this possible.

In the end, we want to stay close to the reality of our embodied human lives, for only the real bears beatitude, grace, and virtue. There is little growth to be had in constantly revisiting our own psychological states. Salvation is not likely to be found in further sensitivity to our thoughts. Rather, we need our thoughts to be saved by having them acted out and put in contact with God and his creation. Sure, there are plenty of ways to fail, but there are far more ways to flourish. With beatitude on our horizon, the grace of God to fill our sails, and the virtue of prudence to steer the course, there are great adventures to be had. To pilot well the ship of our lives, we need only be a little bold. The rest takes care of itself.

Reflect

Recall a few recent questions of conscience you tried to sort out. In trying to resolve them, how did you go about informing your conscience? How did knowing the facts help you in your choice?

Sticking with those same questions, how did you go about motivating your actions? How did virtue help you in your choice?

How would you characterize your current approach to regular confession? What role does prudence play in your preparation and practice? How might a prudence-centered mentality help you to draw more from the sacrament?

7

Am I Certain?

In practical matters, we are always happening upon the one-in-a-million and the could-have-been-otherwise. These encounters introduce uncertainty into our choices. Having only explored a few options, aren't we bound to wonder if the best may be found elsewhere? How can we know that we've seen all that there is to see? This is a real fear that many experience. Fortunately, it's a fear that prudence addresses. How? By insisting on the difference between what we can know and what we can't, and by seeking the certainty of a virtuous life squarely within the bounds of human possibility.

How then are we to proceed? Furthermore, what are we to do with our uncertainty? Should we hold off on the decision until we're really sure? Or open the Bible randomly and look for a sign? Or something else entirely? The answer has become familiar by this point. If we want to choose well and be certain, we have to grow in prudence. This means, first, cultivating genuine moral maturity — persevering in prayer, making good use of the sacraments, seeking to grow in virtue, introducing some penance in your life, cultivating healthy friendships, studying the faith. It also means reimagining what we mean by certainty. Decision-making simply has to get away from evaluating tortured psychological states. The "correct" answer isn't a matter of performing the right mental gymnastics. Decision-making will continue to remain difficult, but that difficulty needn't disconcert us. Rather, it ought to draw out an increasingly free and generous response. And, since prudence perfects our use of practical reason, making us both whole and bold, it is the key for bringing about this transformation and readying us for a life of concrete choices. Only in this way do we derive certainty.

In short, we don't need to know everything there is to be known about a choice before we choose. The only prerequisites are knowing what can be known and acting in accord with virtue. Prudence, with the certainty it affords, accomplishes both of these things. Ultimately, the goal of a prudent life isn't to avoid all mistakes or to guarantee all successes; it's to live one's life well and become a saint. As it turns out, a touch of uncertainty and a glut of errors are entirely consistent with that goal. This side of eternity, we can only achieve the uncertain certainty of prudence, but that's enough to choose well and to do the good with what we've got.

A Bold Certainty for the Whole of Life

There are different kinds of certainty to be had in life, depending upon what kind of knowledge we're working with. Usually, when we think of certainty, we think of absolute or mathematical certainty, sometimes called speculative certainty. This is the certainty we have that 2 + 2 = 4. This is the domain of the virtues of understanding, knowledge, and wisdom. Prudence can't give this kind of certainty, because it doesn't deal with the same subject matter. Prudence deals with the uncertain truths of human action. The certainty it gives is an uncertain certainty, sometimes called moral or practical certainty. Moral certainty is basically the certainty we have of something that happens *for the most part.*

Moral certainty is the certainty that a jury is looking for before they rule on the guilt of the defendant. As they hear a variety of witnesses, they are looking to find a preponderance of evidence. Once they have it, they can be certain of their ruling. Prudence works a bit like this. Prudence's certainty, though, is not based on the testimony of witnesses. Rather, it's based on the testimony of the moral virtues. Effectively, when lining up an action, prudence checks in with justice, fortitude, and temperance. The prudent person asks, would a just, courageous, and temperate person perform this action? If the answer is yes, then he or she can be certain. That's roughly all that moral certainty entails. Why, though, the testimony of the moral virtues? Why not something else?

The moral virtues give prudence its principles for action. As we have seen, the moral virtues clarify our appetites, providing us with insight into human goods. As the moral virtues make us to be better, they cause us to see better, and with that comes certainty. The more robust our formation in the moral virtues, the more certain is our footing in practical matters. Take the example of a battlefield commander. Neither a cowardly nor a rash captain has surety of his commands. A cowardly captain can't be certain when he thinks his company should retreat. His inclination might just indicate that he lacks the fortitude to take the requisite measures. The rash captain can't be certain of his action either. He may feel impelled to take a risk, but, then again, he always does. Perhaps he simply doesn't value his life or the lives of his soldiers. A courageous captain, though, can afford to be certain. He knows that he wouldn't ask anything of his soldiers that he doesn't first ask of himself. He also is able to see what is called for in the circumstances. As a result, he sets out boldly. In the case of the captain, moral virtue is the key to moral certainty. When he knows that his action arises from a courageous character, he can be certain that it is a prudent course.

Not only does prudence take its cue from the moral virtues when formulating the action, it also checks in with the moral virtues when performing the action. In this exchange, the moral virtues let prudence know whether its judgment is sound or not. If it is sound, the judgment translates to virtuous action. If it isn't, then it doesn't. Take the example of a soon-to-be college graduate. She has big plans for the future. She wants to make it as a writer, launch a periodical, and work for social change. At this point though, she doesn't know how best to go about it. Should she look for jobs in creative writing? Should she apply to graduate school? Because her path will be arduous and long, it's hard to say which will contribute best to the realization of her big plans. Still, she can have a kind of certainty. She knows that if she is going to succeed, she will have to grow in virtue. She will have to grow in truthfulness (justice), magnanimity and perseverance (fortitude), and humility (temperance) — just to name a few. With this in mind, she can approach her decision with an eye toward growth. Which will challenge her more, contribute more to her formation in character? Ultimately, she can be certain of her choice, provided it is just, courageous, and temperate. Here, again, moral virtue is the key to moral certainty. When she knows that her action bears out and contributes to a just, courageous, and temperate character, she can be certain that it is a prudent course.

Prudence is situated "between" the moral virtues. On the one hand, prudence receives its principles from the moral virtues. The more morally virtuous one is, the clearer those principles are. On the other hand, prudence applies its judgments to the moral virtues. The more prudent one is, the more consistently one's judgments translate to morally virtuous action. Prudence and the moral virtues are mutually reinforcing. They grow together. Where the moral virtues are, there too is prudence. As a result, the moral virtues secure prudence's objectivity. In answer to the question, "Is this a prudent choice?" one can respond with greater certainty provided that he or she is just, courageous, and temperate. The key to prudence's certainty is the unity and integrity of the human person ordered to action by a life of virtue.

The Correct Answer

Notice that this doesn't mean that one is always searching for a single correct answer. In fact, it leaves a lot of room for variety. Prudence isn't bound to a hypothetical best possible state of affairs. Instead, it seeks what fits with a virtuous character. The goal is to choose means that accord with virtue and promote virtue. There are always better and worse means to a given end. Of course, one seeks to identify the best, but it may not always present itself. Say, for instance, that you're choosing a Christmas present for your goddaughter. You ask her mom what she wants. You ask her what she wants. You shop around, make purchases, wrap the gifts, and present them. As she opens them up, it's clear that, while not displeased, she's not blown away. You got some B+ gifts. Better luck next year. After the fact, you can evaluate whether there were better options, and maybe you approach it differently next year. Frankly, though, the main point is that you love your goddaughter and that

> **Prudence isn't bound to a hypothetical best possible state of affairs. Instead, it seeks what fits with a virtuous character.**

your gifts tried to convey that. That's enough.

The prudent person can't treat morality as if it were a deductive science. Human life is too complex, and it takes more than intelligence to figure it out. Truth be told, trying to get the correct answer in every choice may actually paralyze prudence. If only the hypothetical, best possible solution were sufficient, you couldn't ever be certain that you had happened upon it. In practical matters, there is simply no speculative certainty to be found. Making a choice isn't like solving a math problem. Certainty in a choice will never be such as to remove all anxiety, and so you have to learn to live with it. All you get in practical matters is the uncertain certainty of prudence. In time though, the life of virtue imparts its own confidence and certainty. Moved by the moral virtues and applied to the moral virtues, prudence's judgment begins to take on the aspect of surety. Ultimately, the real human certainty derived from prudence lies in its power to make one good.

Think of how this applies to Natural Family Planning. How do a mother and father know for sure that they are ready to welcome another child? Short answer: They don't. Long answer: Couples may consider a variety of reasons for waiting to conceive. There may be serious financial constraints; they may have children with special needs who demand much of their energy; the mother may have grave complications with each pregnancy. In their thought and prayer, they weigh these factors prudently, with an openness to God's will, and eventually come to a decision. Still, they will never be absolutely certain of their choice.

If they seek such certainty, they may risk *overplanning* in search of the hypothetical, best possible solution. Whatever they choose though, when they choose prudently, will give them sufficient surety. Though they cannot know beyond any shadow of a doubt, they can know enough. Their family plan will not disappoint, provided only that it is shaped by virtue and genuinely open to life.

We are responsible for becoming good and acting well. We are not responsible for weighing every possible factor that may contribute to a choice. We can neither know those factors nor act upon them. Limitation is baked into our human reality. Acknowledging and accepting that fact doesn't amount to resignation; it is actually a source of empowerment. Consent to the limitations of what prudence can and cannot do brings with it the wholeness and boldness of real human certainty.

The Bounds of Certainty

Human certainty comes from what we can really know, but in practical matters there are a lot of unknowns. Real certainty is found within those limits, within the terms set for us by our actual lives. When it comes to limits, we first have to be reconciled to the inscrutability of human affairs. In a given situation, there are any number of ways that you can legitimately act. And with each of these ways, there are potential consequences, both good and bad. Once you begin to entertain all of these consequences, the prospect of making a decision may become overwhelming.

For instance, let's say that a friend recently hosted you

for the weekend while you were in town for business. You are grateful and want to communicate that. You could buy her a little house plant, for instance, or give her a gift certificate to a local restaurant. In truth these are both good options. But might there not also be unforeseen complications that render them unfitting? On the one hand, she might be hyper-pragmatic and see a house plant as just something else to take care of in her already busy life. On the other hand, she might see a gift certificate as evidence that you're not comfortable receiving without repaying, causing her to question the authenticity of the friendship. So, what do you do? Get bent out of shape at the thought that she might be less than pleased and choose to do nothing? No. The point is that you do something that expresses your appreciation and attempts to deepen your friendship. Depending on how well you know her, you might be able to anticipate potential sensitivities, but you also might not. You can only act on what you can know. You are not responsible for reading her mind, and it's not reasonable to expect that of yourself. What is reasonable is that you act virtuously. Provided that you do, you can be certain that the act is good. Might it have bad consequences? Perhaps, but truth be told, that's not your business.

Even though human affairs are inscrutable, we have what we need for choosing well. Prudence sees to that. First, it gathers the variety of our moral experience, drawing upon our successes and failures and taking its cues from law and grace, custom and culture. Then, it condenses that experience into a rough working model, one reflecting what happens always or for the most part, which then serves as the basis for present and future endeavors. This working model gets the job done as well as it can be done. Errors crop up, but they're rare. In the case of selecting a gift for your host, your response is shaped in part by your virtuous formation, by the setting in which you live, and by the peculiarities of this particular friendship. For most people, a small gift will do the trick perfectly. Every once in a while, you'll be thrown for a loop, but you needn't brace yourself against that chance occurrence. You take it in stride.

Practically speaking, we cannot live in perpetual fear of the consequences of our choices, nor permit them to keep us from acting. Negative consequences will inevitably arise from our decisions. This is especially true when it means confrontation with another person. Perhaps you are thinking about suggesting to your friend that he see a counselor or therapist, but what if he takes it the wrong way? Or maybe you are thinking about alerting your boss to some financial irregularities, but what if some of your colleagues get fired? What do you do?

If you are dedicated to living in truth and abiding in love, it's practically guaranteed that you will upset other people. That's very stressful, but it shouldn't keep you from acting. You are genuinely able to testify to the truth and encourage others in virtue. You may be uncertain of your ability to do so, but you can't let that get in the way. With each interaction of this sort, you can simply ask yourself: "Does this actually matter? Can this actually change? Am

I actually motivated by love?" If the answer to those questions is yes, then it's just a matter of timing. Do your best, and don't beat yourself up if the other person reacts poorly.

Over the course of a lifetime, interactions like this should get easier, and occasions of stress and perplexity fewer. As your working model gets fine-tuned, it draws more readily from a richer store of experience. This isn't simply to say that by experiencing more things, you will automatically become more prudent. There are plenty of "experienced" people who live imprudently until their last breath. This goes back to the integral part of memory. What is important isn't so much a breadth of experience as a depth of experience. The prudent individual might never leave his zip code, but he can nonetheless discover what is in the heart of man. So, while he might not see everything there is to see, he can come in time to experience everything there is to experience. With that comes a greater moral certainty, even in difficult encounters. That is what lies in store. That is what is expected of us.

That accounts, then, for the things below us — the inscrutability of human affairs. But, what about the things above? Many experience God's designs as maddeningly mysterious. The Psalmist sings, "Such knowledge is too wonderful for me; / it is high, I cannot attain it" (Ps 139:6). Saint Paul muses, "O the depth of the riches and wisdom and knowledge of God! How unsearchable are his judgments and how inscrutable his ways!" (Rom 11:33). God's ways are so far beyond us. Despite our best efforts, they seem to always elude us. Though one might peer behind the veil at times, the common lot is one of general bewilderment. To what extent, then, can we really know his plan?

Imagine someone who reasons about a decision along the following lines: God is eternal, so he sees everything — past, present, and future — in one gaze. In that one gaze, he sees my life, my future, my flourishing. God knows it all. What is more, he knows this choice — how it should go, how it will go. But, for whatever reason, God has not seen fit to reveal to me what he knows. Perhaps he will reveal it at some future date. In the meantime, everything else remains on hold. After all, I don't want to mess it up.

While some of this thinking is true, it represents a flawed way of understanding and interpreting God's providence. What is more, if endorsed, it can seriously hamstring our efforts at living a virtuous life. There are four basic tenets at work in this position:

1. God knows the plan.
2. I am capable of knowing the plan.
3. In order to act, I need to know the plan.
4. It's up to me to know the plan and to act upon it.

Each tenet is true on the surface, but underneath a few of them is just enough error to skew one's understanding of divine providence.

God knows the plan.

If God created it, he knows it. Since he created it all, he knows it all. Since God is the author of all creation, his providence encompasses every imaginable aspect of things visible and invisible. Nothing escapes his gaze. There's nothing here that's objectionable.

I am capable of knowing the plan.

Indeed, we have intellectual natures capable of receiving God's revelation. By faith God gives us his very own knowledge of himself. Faith, though, is a virtue on the way. "Faith is the assurance of things *hoped for*, the conviction of *things not seen*" (Heb 11:1). Faith isn't yet the vision of heaven. "For now we see in a mirror dimly, but then face to face" (1 Cor 13:12). While on earth, there will always be limits to what we know. Even in heaven, we still won't know the plan exactly as God does. To comprehend the plan perfectly, we would have to comprehend God perfectly. But God is infinitely greater than our minds and hearts. As human beings, we can only know his plan to a limited extent, according to our limited capacity.

In order to act, I need to know the plan.

It's true that we can't choose what we don't know, but we don't need to know all of the details, just some of them. We need to know what pertains to us, and that is for God to decide. Often enough, God chooses to show us the next step and little else. We have to be content with that. As St. John Henry Newman writes:

> Lead, Kindly Light, amid the encircling gloom
> > Lead Thou me on!
> The night is dark, and I am far from home—
> > Lead Thou me on!
> Keep Thou my feet; I do not ask to see
> The distant scene—one step enough for me.

One step is enough. While it might be nice to have a sense for the whole of one's life within the broad sweep of salvation history, such vision awaits us only at the general resurrection. As for now, "Thy word is a lamp to my feet / and a light to my path" (Ps 119:105).

It's up to me to know the plan and to act upon it.

The healthy emphasis on acting is well-placed, but we often look in the wrong direction for marching orders. Many people seem to think that they can't proceed without explicit directions. "I'll do whatever you ask of me Lord, I just don't know what it is." But God's plans are not often communicated with crystalline clarity, like the onrush of prophetic insight. Instead, they are given in the quiet certainty of prudence:

God's plans are not often communicated with crystalline clarity, like the onrush of prophetic insight. Instead, they are given in the quiet certainty of prudence.

> For this commandment which I command you

this day is not too hard for you, neither is it far off. It is not in heaven, that you should say, 'Who will go up for us to heaven, and bring it to us, that we may hear it and do it?' Neither is it beyond the sea, that you should say, 'Who will go over the sea for us, and bring it to us, that we may hear it and do it?' But the word is very near you; it is in your mouth and in your heart, so that you can do it. (Deuteronomy 30:11–14)

God's plans are at work in our own ability and desire. They arise organically from the outworking of the life of grace and virtue.

God alone sees the plan in its plenitude. It is for him to give and for us to receive, and we receive it by prudence. Prudence is just our created share in God's providence. By providence, God takes care of the whole world, orchestrating the movements of all the creatures that fall within his power. Some of those creatures fail; some of those creatures sin; but God is able to incorporate even failure and sin into a work of great glory. By prudence, we take care of our world, orchestrating the movements of everything that falls within our power. Sometimes we fail; sometimes we sin; but we, by God's grace, are able to incorporate even failure and sin into a work of great glory.

Prudence gives us the insight to see who we are and where we fit, helping us to flourish within the bounds of human limitations. Prudence empowers us to know our part and to play it well. Think of human life as a role in a stage play. The actors in the play need to know something of the playwright's intention and the director's vision to interpret their part well, but they don't need to know all the details. They just need to be good actors. If an actress felt that she had to know what Shakespeare had for breakfast on the morning of April 29, 1578, and the precise reason why he named his children as he did before acting the part of Desdemona, that'd be a bit excessive. Certainly she needs to know something of the context and setting of *Othello*, but not all there is to know. She needs to know her movements and her lines, and she needs to deliver them beautifully. So too in human life. Like the actress, we have enough to go on. Sure, we may not know the whole of God's plan, but, frankly, we don't need to. We were made to learn our movements and our lines and to deliver them beautifully. While we may chafe at being so bound, we can be certain that the script is good and that it leaves nothing out. What is more, we are amateurs, and so we can't reasonably expect to deliver our lines flawlessly. We can reasonably expect to deliver them with our best effort, recognizing that our every word and work is under the care of he who is at once playwright, director, and principal actor. And so we needn't call the play into question or write our own. We trust that we've tried our best to do the good and that our happiness lies in just such a pursuit.

Choices, Quandaries, and the Good Life

Though the inscrutability of human affairs and the mysteriousness of divine providence may give rise to frustration at times, it is within these bounds that we find freedom and certainty. To say, though, that these bounds are good isn't to say that all bounds are good. The limits to our knowledge of human affairs and of divine providence are part of being human. They are given by God, by reality. We receive them; we don't invent them. In addition to the bounds that we receive, though, there are other bounds that we invent for ourselves. Some are good: "I have to stop rebound dating. I'll give myself at least a month after each relationship." "I can't accumulate any more debt. I'm freezing the credit cards and dealing in cash." Some are bad: "I don't really keep up with friends; it's a detachment thing." "This sin, it seems, will be with me until I die." Bounds of this sort impose false limits on life and make it harder to find freedom and certainty. To flourish, we need to address these falsehoods, specifically those that surround our choices.

On a particular day, you might do any number of things: wake up, brush your teeth, take a shower, eat breakfast, go to work, plug away at spreadsheets, drink coffee, check emails, take a few calls, go to Mass, go back to work, sit in on some meetings, update your computer, check the news, sit in traffic, prepare dinner, watch a show, pray a bit, think about the next day, and go to bed. In the course of the day, you may only make a couple of momentous choices where you work through the three acts of counsel, judgment, and command in a conscious way. Do I go to midday Mass or work through lunch? Do I ask my boss about a raise or do I put off the conversation?

Because these kinds of choices occur only at intervals, we often experience them as perplexing. We feel surprised by them or impressed by their consequence. Though we choose all day long, most of the time we know perfectly well what we should do or recognize the choice as a mere matter of preference. Why is it then that these momentous choices stress us out so much? Have we put them in a different category? Have we labeled them as meaningful and the other choices as unmeaningful? Have we bounded our experience such that everything seems to hang on a few choices that matter?

Strangely enough, the best way to choose well in these instances is not by doubling down and reaffirming your resolve. In fact, it's probably not healthy to assign any more importance to these momentous choices than you already have. By focusing too narrowly on them, we risk imposing an artificial bound on our experience, that of limiting our "moral lives" to the occasional and infrequent. Even if only slight, there is a subtle snare at work in this logic. Often, those who entertain it start to believe that their lives aren't really meaningful except at crisis points, as if there were but two settings: cruise control and chase scene. This is an artificial boundary, a false characterization of the moral life, and by conceiving of our choice in this way, we miss out on all the joy of living.

The moral life and its resources are not intended exclusively for crunch time, nor are they addressed principally to solving one's most difficult problems. The meaning of our moral lives is distributed among the various experiences that make up our daily fare. The moral life is not first about problems; it is first about persons. How we make a choice (how we even approach a choice in the first place, for that matter) is a fruit of who we are and who we want to become.

In any decision, the question is not so much about whether I do this or that, but who I am before this choice and who I want to be on the other side of it. One's life isn't principally about results to be realized in the world. That's the domain of the artist. An artist is successful if he makes good and beautiful things, and his standing as an artist is relative to the things made. When it comes to the prudent person though, one's standing as a human being is relative to character. A person is successful if he or she becomes good and noble. The results, the consequences of action, are, in a certain sense, beside the point. As St. Teresa of Calcutta once said, "God has not called me to be success-ful; He has called me to be faithful."

Within this setting, the big choices assume the right kind of importance. They are part of the story of who we are and who we are to become, but just part of the story. Beyond the bounds of the momentous choices, there is a whole moral universe in which to grow as a person and fill out what is lacking in character. From this vantage, we see that we aren't just helpless individuals stumbling from isolated bewildering choice to isolated bewildering choice. We actually shape our future choices, both in how they are presented and in how they are resolved.

Our choices are shaped by our character, and our character gives us the certainty we need. We will never be sure beyond any shadow of a doubt, but neither should we seek to be so. There is much we do not know, but there is also much that we do. We are not robots operating by machine logic. We are human beings acting by prudential logic, which is our small share in God's perfectly providential logic. While cultivating a virtuous life, we can grow ever more rooted in the uncertain certainty of prudence that empowers us to live courageously the life set before us. Before the choices of your life, both great and small, ask not whether it is the theoretically best possible decision or one completely void of bad consequences. Ask instead whether it is good with what you've got. Ask whether it makes you and those whom you love to be good, too.

Reflect

Think back to a good choice you've made. What identified it as a good choice before, during, or after? In the future, how might you be able to better identify the certainty that prudence affords in your practical decision making?

Are there any bounds you have set for your life which you suspect may be false? Have you cordoned off your important choices in some way? What are some steps to reclaiming the whole of your life for happiness and holiness?

Can you think of a choice you have been deferring for a while? Are you conscious of the reasons why you have been deferring it? Are there aspects of the choice or its consequences that you fear? How might this choice offer an opportunity for new-found freedom and certainty?

8

Am I Confident?

With certainty ought to come confidence, a bold exercise of freedom. Why then does it often feel more like we're bluffing rather than actually enjoying that confidence? Why does freedom seem so burdensome? At times it may feel like too much is left up to our freedom, and with this comes bewilderment. Other times it may feel like too little is left up to our freedom, and with this comes discouragement. In either case there arises fear of failure and hesitancy to act. The key to confidence, then, lies in identifying our true freedom and working within its bounds. Ultimately, knowing how freedom is framed helps to understand how freedom is exercised, both in the ordinary day-to-day and in the more extraordinary moments of life.

What does it mean to be free? Many people associate their freedom with independence or with license to do what they want. My freedom ends where your freedom begins. With this understanding, however, the influence of others is seen as a limit to freedom. I am only free to the extent that I set myself up against family, nation, Church, or whomever. Otherwise, I am just another follower. It's in this spirit that many seek to define themselves as unique or special according to their own lights. The question arises: What if I don't know exactly who I am or what I want? What if the encouragement "You be you" leaves me perplexed rather than impassioned? According to a Christian worldview, you needn't fear. There is freedom to be found within the limits of your life.

Receiving Our Freedom

In the traditional understanding, freedom is just as much received as it is exercised. In reality, much of who we are is visited upon us. Take the example of family life. You were born to these parents at this time and place. You were taught a particular language and raised with certain beliefs. By nature and nurture, you have this temperament and this personality. As a result, you are better suited for this work or this vocation. It might seem like this passivity compromises your freedom, but such is not the case. It is, in part, the source of your freedom.

Freedom, we said earlier, is about being a virtuoso human being, one wholly in possession of his humanity. The free person knows his goal in life and will not be deflected from that purpose. In his pursuit of the goal, there are some things that others choose for him and some things that he chooses for himself. Whether those choices come from without or from within is less important; what is more important is that they shape his pursuit of the goal.

The givens of life do not detract from our freedom. They situate it. By ordering us toward a particular version of the good life, these givens establish how we are to flourish. At a certain point, you learned English. That continues to shape how you see reality and how you communicate. You live in the twenty-first century. You won't ever work as a newspaper crier, but you will have to be at least a little tech savvy. And if you were baptized, you have an indelible mark on your soul. That gives you a permanent share in the priesthood of Christ tending always to the worship of God. Before you ever choose, you are fixed as this person in this setting with this life. These factors define what it means for you to live well. Accordingly, you're free to choose what lies within your power, and you needn't bother with what doesn't.

This Christian understanding of freedom may sound unreasonable to those who encounter it for the first time. For instance, what if one's setting is outdated or limited or prejudiced? Shouldn't it be called into question? Perhaps. At times, one may have to rise above his or her setting or even reject it altogether, but this isn't the default position. The default position is to learn from it and work within it, because there may be real wisdom in what we receive.

The givens in life afford us access to the wisdom of

others. They initiate us into a more broadly reasonable life at work in our family, nation, Church, and so on. By welcoming the influence of a childhood mentor, a family tradition, or an ecclesial law, we inherit something of their freedom. By looking to our forebears, we draw strength to choose the kind of life we know to have been good for them. For instance, plenty of young people enlist in the armed services at the age of eighteen. How do they adequately weigh the consequences of that choice? Well, often they don't; but perhaps they don't always need to. A nation needs good soldiers, and it's good to serve one's country. If a father or an uncle served before, that may be enough to fix a boy's mind on it for himself. That's not unreasonable. In fact, it's free.

To choose in this way means to broaden the horizon of choice. Prudence isn't limited to the steps of counsel, judgment, and command. It's at work in our genes, in our language, in our worship. We take part in a reasonable culture in which all kinds of relationships and institutions play their part. With this comes the relief that we don't always have to be anxiously, intentionally, optimally rational. We live the way we do, dress the way we do, believe the way we do in large part because we are borne on by the reasons of others, by our part in the whole. And that is perfectly reasonable. So, why did Christen become an accountant? In part because her father is an accountant. That's a good reason. Why did Regina join this parish? In part because that's where she lived. That's eminently sane.

The secular age would have you believe that reality is

wholly unintelligible, that life only has the meaning you give it. To think so is tempting, especially as traditional institutions and narratives break down. But there is no need to invent the meaning of our situation, and to try to do so is counterproductive, even anti-Christian. Life isn't something that we make up. It's something that we receive. God put you here and now, with this personal, familial, and societal history. He isn't surprised that you are limited and that your reasoning is limited. Not only is that permissible, it's intended. Your freedom is engaged by embracing it.

Exercising Our Freedom

This idea of freedom, as both choosing and receiving, might upset our notion of what it means to be in control. One might protest: "If I don't choose it, then I don't want any part of it!" But such a spirit runs completely counter to the logic of creation and redemption. If we are honest, we have received everything from the hand of God: "What have you that you did not receive? If then you received it, why do you boast as if it were not a gift?" (1 Cor 4:7). Before the givenness of life, the Christian response is not one of dissent, but one of consent, even abandonment.

This idea of consent is premised on a basic truth: God loves you and provides for you. Some things he gives you through your exercise of choice. Some things he gives you through a choice that goes before you. Whether by choosing or receiving, though, God is loving and providing.

God did not create you to no end, for he makes nothing in vain, and you can rely on him to supply you with what you need to flourish. What is more, God has created you for a meaningful pursuit within *this reality*. This is the setting in which your flourishing is to be found. Admittedly, it's one marred by evil, but God would not have permitted that evil were he not able to draw from it some good. What you need to flourish is not to be discovered by going over, under, or around your present circumstances. Rather, it is to be found in willingly embracing them. Real life is not elsewhere. It is here and now.

Imagine that you are a single mother. Your husband recently passed away, and you have two small children. You really want your children to mature in their faith and persevere in their practice of it. You have also heard that having a churchgoing father is the single best predictor for post-collegiate church attendance. What should you do? Remarry for the sake of the children? Try to play the role of the father yourself? Despair entirely? Freedom in this situation amounts to consent: You can only be the children's mother, so be their mother. It may be harder for your children to come to know and love the faith given the loss of their father, but that's beyond your control. You are only free to be you — a good woman and good mother — once you accept that.

So, what then are you responsible for? Saint Augustine prays, "God give what you command and command what you will." God will supply you with what you need for the life to which he has appointed you, a life crafted in the depths of his wisdom and animated by his boundless mercy. Its unfolding will look different than that of the next person, but you can embrace it with the confidence that it is good and that it is yours. Only you are able to reveal what God's grace can do in the here and now of your life. By offering your consent to life as God gives it, you become a monstrance of his peculiar love and announce something unique of his divine life.

Only you are able to reveal what God's grace can do in the here and now of your life.

At the heart of his will for your life, you have real freedom. Since God's eternal plan includes you and your actions, you may be tempted to think that your life is predetermined. But his plan is so powerful that, not only does he cause you to act, he causes you to act *freely.* God's creative power does not force our hand or act violently on our liberty. He moves us strongly and sweetly in a way more interior to us than we are to ourselves. He makes our acts to arise naturally and organically as the fruit of our choice. So, yes, God sees your future which is eternally present to him, but he sees it as something he brings about *in and through* your act of free choice. In accounting for everything, his plan accounts for (and makes possible) your very contribution.

How do you contribute? By playing the hand you're dealt and playing it as well as you know how. Your life may not seem the best, but you can be confident that God's plan is good. The best life for you is the life that God actually gives. It is the product of his love, and he loves you quite a bit — more than you love yourself, more than you could ever imagine. The hand you've been dealt is a hand dealt by love. God wants you to be happy more than you do. He wants you to be a saint more than you do. With this in mind, it's possible to play your hand with a kind of joy and, in the playing of it, to become good. God is not waiting for you to mess up. He is excited to see you and to cause you to live beautifully, truly, and well.

Ordinary Freedom

So how then do we exercise this freedom? The last four chapters have each already responded to this question in one way or another. Here, we'll limit what remains to some very practical advice, treating first the ordinary and then the extraordinary exercise of our freedom.

In an ordinary choice, begin by consulting your desires. Who are *you*, and what do you *really* love? It's good that you want to do God's will, but how does his will take root in your humanity? Take your cues from what draws you. It's like choosing at a diner. You have a huge menu before you, so you start with the normal questions: What have I been hankering for? Am I thinking sweet or savory? Do I want to bring home leftovers for dinner? Do I want to feel good about my life afterwards or like I have a rock in my stomach? It'd be strange to ask what God wants you to order and leave it at that. You answer that question by thinking virtuously and picking something. Because desire is God-given, you can trust it, and as you grow in grace, you can trust it more. Note: There's no sense in choosing something more difficult if it's not for you. God isn't interested in what you think is hard. God is interested in what you love. The principle of merit is charity, not exertion. He created you and redeemed you for love, not for drudgery. So, tend toward what you love and, as you do, your virtuous inclinations will take more definite shape.

God isn't interested in what you think is hard. God is interested in what you love.

At this stage, you will always be dealing with mixed motivations. "Okay, I want the number four, but there's no way I'll finish it. That being said, I can take the rest home. Also, he's paying, so there's that, as well." Because we are fallen people with fallen powers, we can't expect to summon perfectly pure motivations at a moment's notice, as in: "I will choose the number seven because it is dietetically balanced, perfectly proportioned, and eminently suited for my day's work of ministering to the poor." This side of heaven, it just doesn't play out that way. And yet, even though our inclinations are weak and wounded, we can still manage to choose well. If you live your life virtuously, your motivations will be purified, but only with time.

Having consulted your desires, next weigh your options. Some options are evil and the choice of them sinful. Obviously, those are to be avoided. Here the moral law helps by giving clear indication of what's out of bounds. There are plenty of good options though, and we're genuinely free to choose among them. You are in search of what is good for you, here and now, given the concrete and particular circumstances of your life. It may *seem* holier to make a holy hour, attend Mass, pray the Liturgy of the Hours, and serve with the Missionaries of Charity every day, but that mode of life is *not* holier for a project manager during the busy season or a young parent currently potty-training the twins. The holy thing is what makes you faithful, charitable, and generally virtuous in your real life. Be confident that God drew you into your vocation because it's the best way of making *you* holy. What you're after is the good option for you, an option which may not always look how you imagined it would, but that is, in fact, good. Only your real life bears grace, not the life that might have been. There are all sorts of paths that lead to sanctity. Take yours.

Also, when weighing options, don't overthink it. Fixating on a choice can be counterproductive. In the discernment of vocation, for instance, you sometimes hear the following: "I would like to marry this man. I hope we will be engaged soon. Sometimes, though, I worry that I haven't discerned sufficiently. Religious life seems like it would be really burdensome for me, even unpleasant. Maybe, though, that's just what I need." It's this type of overthinking that gets us all bound up. If your head causes you to sin, cut it off and cast it from you (See Mt 5:29-30, sort of). Often enough, you know what to do. Trust yourself. God does.

Next, do the thing. Prudent thought should lead to prudent action. Some may be tempted to second guess or defer to another day. Others might be tempted to launch into action without taking counsel or making sound judgments. Virtue is not too much and not too little. Virtue, Aristotle writes, is in the middle. It's in the mean. Think it through, then see it through. If you're an indecisive person, you might practice making small decisions within a set limit of time, whether it's choosing a new show or selecting a rest stop to gas up. Limit your options to quell your fears. You could also try choosing the thing you're immediately drawn to in order to see what happens. You may be pleased to discover that your instincts are good. If you're an excessively decisive person, practice deferring to someone else's judgment from time to time or asking for input from a friend or family member, even if you feel like you don't need it. Try to take their advice every so often. You might also make small journal entries of decisions and read them after a few weeks to see how your original confidence has matured.

Finally, assess how you did. Often, we think about prudence at work before the act and in the act, but prudence is also at work after the act in the work of assessment. That assessment needn't be overly complicated. How did it go? Were you pleased with the result? What did you learn? Whatever you do, though, assessment shouldn't be reduced to simple self-accusation or self-justification. It's not just about whether you got it right or wrong. It's about growing from your successes and failures. The hope is that, by this practice, you cultivate self-knowledge and move in the direction of genuine self-acceptance. Apparently, for better or worse, this is who you are. With self-acceptance, then, comes self-transcendence. When you really know who you are, you are less surprised by your failings and weaknesses and better disposed to offer them to God.

In the work of assessment, it can be easy to get lost in our own heads, and so it's good to have recourse to friends. Friends encourage us in the virtuous life: They both model it for us and talk us through it. They widen and deepen our insights. They see things that we don't. We're often inclined to give the best interpretation of our own actions and the worst of others. Friends aren't so easily fooled. Knowing us and loving us as they do, though, they are able to communicate the truth in a way that is both candid and gentle. If you find that your friends are reticent to offer their advice or correction, consider giving them your explicit encouragement to do so. While their input may be painful at times, it is a great help to growth in prudence.

We can also enrich our assessment by reading good literature. Prudence, we have said, comes from experience. When we read literature, we share in the author's experience of human life. While engrossed in good literature, we live in the characters' heads, partake of their action, and see succinctly how their lives play out. Within the arc of the plot, we are able to draw connections between their activity and destiny, their choices and their flourishing. By reading good literature, we can profit from rich insights into humanity, and those insights can transform our own approach to human life.

Human life itself has a kind of narrative quality. Our

lives are stories in the telling. Part of our energies are devoted to living that story. Part of our energies are devoted to interpreting it. By interpreting it well, we are empowered to live better. Self-reflection, the company of friends, and the riches of literature are all part of this work. Each helps us to better consent to the story that God is recounting in us, rather than searching idly for a different tale. In the end, you can be confident that the story is good, for it is yours, and God has chosen to tell it through you and you alone.

Extraordinary Freedom

It's one thing to be confident in the ordinary day-to-day of prudent living, but what about the extraordinary times which seem entirely beyond us? Regardless of how prudent we are, there are bound to be certain decisions that leave us baffled. Say you work at a pharmaceutical company on the HR side. You don't always understand the research side, but you're beginning to think that some of the current projects are a bit dubious. That being said, you've just had your third child in five years, and things are a bit tight financially. It would not be a good time to change companies, especially with the industry in its current state. What should you do?

When thinking through a concrete choice, we ordinarily rely upon our human wherewithal. We consult experience (memory), ask advice (docility), weigh principles (understanding), intuit consequences (shrewdness), and reason it out (reasoning). Sometimes, though, that human wherewithal just isn't enough. The choice is just too big, too difficult, too obscure. In these moments, we may feel despondent. Curiously enough, though, it is in these moments that God is nearest. Recall what was said earlier of the gifts of the Holy Spirit. When the virtues are stretched to their limits, the gifts come to their aid. When the virtues falter from human deficiency, the gifts lift them to a divine sufficiency.

When prudence, in particular, comes up against obstacles, the Holy Spirit intercedes through the gift of *counsel.* Counsel supplies us the extraordinary wisdom of God's prudence, one far surpassing the ordinary wisdom of our own. You can think of prudence as a young physician who is attending a patient with strange symptoms, symptoms that don't conform to any diagnosis known to him. This physician may know a great deal, he may be the brightest of his generation, but there are bound to be cases that fall outside his expertise. When such a case arises, he consults a senior physician who has seen it all and who can make a clear diagnosis. Counsel is like the senior physician. This doesn't suggest that prudence is faulty. It's just limited. And in those moments, it appeals to the limitless wisdom of God.

It's hard to describe exactly how the Spirit communicates this wisdom. Some spiritual authors describe it as a kind of affective or heart knowledge. Others explain it as a sweet and intimate experience of divine wisdom, like "having the eyes of your hearts enlightened" (Eph 1:18). In counsel, God doesn't so much communicate, step-by-step, how things are going to go. Rather, he causes the soul to see as he does. He imparts a savor for his divine plan and for our place within it, and he gives us an instinct for faithfully and charitably carrying it out. The gift of counsel causes the soul to sing, "I will run in the way of thy commandments / when thou enlargest my understanding!" (Ps 119:32).

Counsel opens us to the divine prompting. It does not so much initiate prudent action, as receive prudent action. Luis Martinez writes in *The Sanctifier* that, "[By counsel, the Holy Spirit] constitutes himself the immediate director of the soul, which in its full strength and freedom moves only under his inspiration."

When you feel yourself confused by a tough choice, you should be on the lookout for the gift of counsel. While certain indications might suggest one solution to your problem, you might feel yourself drawn to another. In that latter direction lies "love, joy, peace, patience, kindness, goodness, faithfulness, gentleness, and self-control" (Gal 5:22-23). There may be plenty of reasons that make it difficult to heed the divine instinct. Perhaps it'd be risky or unpopular or even silly. Don't be discouraged. As you begin to follow the Spirit's cue, it gets easier to identify his inspirations and follow them in the future.

Though exercised often in extraordinary circumstances, counsel is a regular part of Christian life. It's given with the grace of baptism. Like the virtue of prudence, it's a habit of mind, which means that it's a stable and permanent disposition to be Spirit-led. It responds to Christ's promise that the Holy Spirit "dwells with you, and will be in you" (Jn 14:17). Ultimately, it's an essential feature of beatitude. For, while prudence is perfect in a way, it relies upon counsel to direct our actions all the way to heaven.

Confident Freedom

With that, we've got the basics of the virtue of prudence. All that remains is to live them. That, though, is still difficult. No sense in saying otherwise. Along the way, there will be stumbling blocks. All of us sin and will continue to do so, despite our best efforts. There will also be humbling disappointments. Not all dreams come true, especially if you dream big. For all that, though, you can be confident that you have what it takes to venture forth.

Admittedly, there is a real gap between the exalted Christian vocation and our weak and wounded natures. That we even dare to pray the "Our Father," C. S. Lewis remarks, is itself astonishing. After all, aren't we putting ourselves in the place of a son or daughter of God? Aren't we dressing up as Christ? Isn't that some pretty preposterous pretending? And yet, it's the startling truth. In baptism God adopted you and commanded you to live accordingly.

So if you still feel yourself to be pretending, remember that some pretending can be good. Children, Lewis comments, pretend to be grown-ups all the time, and, before too long, they get the hang of it. So too in the moral life. Lewis writes in *Mere Christianity*, "When you are not feeling particularly friendly but know you ought to be, the best thing you can do, very often, is to put on a friendly manner and behave as if you were a nicer person than you actually are. And in a few minutes, as we have all noticed, you will be really feeling friendlier than you were. Very often the only way to get a quality in reality is to start behaving as if you had it already."

For those, then, who remain overwhelmed at the prospect of choosing well, of living life as a prudent risk, you can afford to be a little confident. Ultimately, "pretending" is just progressing. Life is like any project. It's imposing in the abstract or at the outset, but it gets easier when you just start doing it. We were made to act. We can and should act. Along the way we will make many, many mistakes. That can be troublesome, but it's the only way to grow. "For a righteous man falls seven times, and rises again" (Prv 24:16).

God doesn't ask us to be perfect yesterday. He asks us to try today. God created us to do marvelous things in a gloriously blundering way. His perfect plan works through our imperfect actions. God knows that our best is limited and flawed, and he loves it. He hasn't somehow lowered his expectations to accommodate our weaknesses and sinfulness. In fact, he makes us rise to him precisely in and through them.

Our life is a life on the way. Though it may feel like a lot, it is possible. Don't let the perfect be the enemy of the good. God gives you enough for the task, and you are enough for the task. God has more confidence in you than you do. The only way you can disappoint him is by despairing of that confidence. So seek to choose him in everything you do, and you will succeed in his eyes, which, in the end, are the eyes that matter.

Reflect

What are some aspects of your life that you wish were otherwise? What about them can be changed and what about them can't? How can accepting the aspects you can't change contribute to greater freedom?

If it's true that your real life isn't elsewhere, that it's here and now, what specifically about your real life do you still need to consent to? What would it mean to play the hand you're dealt in these circumstances?

Think again of a choice that you have been putting off. What do you suspect you really want to do? What is keeping you from pursuing that course? Challenge yourself to move forward confidently in prudence.